THE MESSIAH STORY

The Promise of God

A delightful and insightful poem connecting
the dots from Genesis to Revelation.

MARIANNE GIBBS SMITH

WestBow Press books may be ordered through booksellers or by contacting:

WestBow Press
A Division of Thomas Nelson & Zondervan
1663 Liberty Drive
Bloomington, IN 47403
www.westbowpress.com
1 (866) 928-1240

ISBN: 978-1-4908-8433-2 (sc)
ISBN: 978-1-4908-8432-5 (e)

Library of Congress Control Number: 2015909592

Print information available on the last page.

WestBow Press rev. date: 8/10/2015

Contents

Keys to the Icons

These icons are included in this poem to tie together the primary subjects recorded in scripture and to point out the connection of Old Testament prophecy and New Testament fulfillment.

Bread and Wine symbolic of the broken body and poured-out blood of the Messiah.

Cross the sacrificial death of the Messiah for the forgiveness of sin.

Dove The Holy Spirit

Lamb The crucified Christ, who provided the blood offering for our sin

Nativity the virgin birth of the Messiah, Bethlehem.

Snake Satan

Star of David Israel, the land of promise that God promised to Abraham, Isaac and Jacob and their descendants and the prophesied location of the Messiah's eternal throne.

Throne The promise of God that the Messiah will be a descendant of King David and will rule forever from King David's Throne in Jerusalem, or Zion,

Wrapped Up in a Baby

It takes the book of Genesis for the Gospel to make sense.
Therefore debunking Genesis has enormous consequence.
It has to do with who we are and why we're really here.
It has to do with knowing love, or being filled with fear.
The Lord God wasn't kidding when he told Adam of His plan
Or when He spoke to Moses of how it all began.
It was the fall of Adam that passed sin on to man.
Affecting all the offspring of his human clan.
Only sinless, human blood can wash the sin away,
And it came wrapped up in a baby on that first Christmas day.

THE OLD TESTAMENT

CREATION

In the beginning God created the heavens and earth;
God's Spirit hovered, preparing for birth.
Then God's word came forth with power and might,
As He declared, "Let there be light!"
He spoke into existence all things that be;
He brought forth the sky, the earth, and the sea.
God made everything for specific reasons;
He made lights in sky for signs and for and seasons.
By His Word He created the moon and the sun;
The animals and plants; and when He was done,
He created His masterpiece to finish His Plan,
In His own image, His masterpiece, Man.
Male and female created He them,
Forever to be companions to Him.
The man's name was Adam, and Eve was his wife;
God planned for them a beautiful life.
God created all-the-above in only six days
And gave Adam the seventh to rest and to praise.
In the beginning God created time, so to speak;
When He was done, He had created the week.

God created Adam in the most interesting way:
He formed the man right out of the clay.
He breathed the Breath of Life into his nose;

Adam came to life from his head to his toes.
Adam possessed great skill with his words;
He named all the animals: the beasts, and the birds.
He performed this job with perfect dispatch
And saw that he did not have a match.
When he fell asleep, God took a rib from his side,
And He formed the woman to become Adam's bride.
Adam exclaimed, "I am no longer alone!
She is flesh of my flesh and bone of my bone."

THE FALL

God gave them dominion over all of the Earth,
A land of abundance and joyous mirth,
To be fruitful, have children, explore, and invent.
A life of blessing was God's only intent.
In the creation we see God's awesome mind--
Teaching the first law of science, each bears its own kind:
"I give you these seeds to plant for your keeping;
This world is established by sowing and reaping.
Seedtime and harvest never will cease;
Man plants the seed, and I give the increase.
In the Garden of Eden with sweet fruit on the trees,
For all of your food, you may eat off of these."
But God gave warning to Adam: "Don't eat from one tree;
It gives knowledge of evil, which is not made for thee.
If you eat of that tree, you surely will die."
Then Satan in snake form told Eve, "That's a lie!
You'll be like God and be ever so wise."
Eve was deceived by the serpent's smooth lies.
Eve believed that sly snake and ate of the tree;
Then Adam ate too, deliberately.
And since that time, as God knew it would,
Man defines for himself what is evil or good.
The way that God made it, the way He had planned,
No sickness or death would be on this land.
Now sin had entered, and death took its hold;

Our lives would be measured, and we would grow old.
Adam and Eve suffered for what they just did;
They grabbed some fig leaves, and then they hid.
God found them hiding in sorrow and shame;
They were both quick to pass on the blame.
From that time on man lived under a curse:
Separated from God; what could be worse!
Because Adam and Eve obeyed Satan's voice,
They lost their dominion by their sad choice.
This beautiful world then became Satan's toy;
He now had the right to kill and destroy.

The Promise

It was at this dark moment in history
That God spoke of His Plan in Genesis three:
"From the seed of a woman, a Man will be born
Who will crush Satan's head and put him to scorn."
(In the Old Testament, God paves the way
And is setting the stage for the first Christmas Day.)
For who would have guessed it, this mysterious plan?
God, Himself, would redeem us by becoming a man.
It was Adam's job to teach God's Plan of Salvation
To be told and retold to each generation.

Consequences

They were cast out of the garden. It was their pay
To eke out a living and make their own way.
God said to Eve she would give birth in pain,
And over her life, her husband would reign.
By the sweat of his brow, Adam would labor and toil.
Then they would die and return to the soil.
God clothed Adam and Eve with coats of skin;
The first blood was shed to cover their sin.

CAIN AND ABEL

Adam and Eve had two sons, Abel and Cain.
By the hand of his brother, Abel was slain.
Abel offered choice lambs to the God he respected.
This was an offering God fully accepted.
Cain then offered some crops from his field.
God was not pleased with his produce and yield.
God then told Cain to offer another,
But Cain resented the success of his brother.
God gave Cain a warning not to be mad
But to come with his gift and be thankful and glad.
This whole correction put Cain in a stew--
When they were out in the field, his brother Cain slew.
God asked Cain, "Where can Abel be found?
For I've heard his blood as it called from the ground."
Then God set a mark upon Cain for protection
And sent him away feeling utter rejection.
After jealous Cain caused Abel's death,
God gave a new son; his name was Seth.
Seth was the one who would start a new line;
Through him would come the Promise divine.

NOAH AND THE FLOOD (2348B.C)

During this time people kept reaping and sowing.
They lived for centuries, and families kept growing.
Nine generations later, the world was so bad,
God's anger was kindled, and He really got mad.
But there was a just man who had made God his choice;
He listened to God and heeded His voice.
This man was Noah, God's trusted one;
God gave him a task, and He knew it'd get done.
God told Noah to warn that judgment would come
And to build a big boat that would hold a large sum.
God gave Noah instructions of what he must do,
For he would be hosting an unusual crew.

Two of each animal that dwelt on the earth
Would need a place on the boat, their own special berth--
Male and female; the small and the large;
The tame and the wild, with Captain Noah in charge,
And also a place for the birds of the air.
The boat must supply perch, stall, and lair.
This Noah did, and it took many years.
The people mocked Noah with laughter and jeers.
God guided the animals in a unique parade
Onto the boat that Noah had made.
Then water poured forth from the earth and the sky,
And all living creatures were destined to die.
The people who laughed were laughing no more,
But it was too late, for God had shut the ark's door.
Noah and his wife were safe on the boat,
And with three sons and their wives, they all stayed afloat.

It rained forty days; then God stopped the rain,
But it took a long time for the water to drain.
The boat settled near the top of Mount Ararat,
And for many months the crew patiently sat.
Three times Noah sent a dove to espy;
When it didn't return, Noah knew all was dry.
It was a year before Noah's God-ordained zoo
Could come off the boat; then life started anew.
Noah's three sons were named Shem, Japheth and Ham.
Shem is the forefather of Abraham.
God told them to multiply and fill up the land,
"And let no human blood be spilled by your hand.
Man is made in My image, and if you do,
The same thing will surely happen to you."

BABEL

Another beginning was now to begin,
But again fallen mankind fell into sin.
Men decided to build a tower so high,

So they could climb clear up to the sky.
Man thought he was clever, all knowing and able,
But God humbled and scattered them at the tower of Babel.
They all spoke one language, and God said, "That's it!
I'll tear down the tower and cause a big split.
If they're all in agreement, with hearts so impure,
They'll bring great destruction; that is for sure."
To confound their ambitions and drive them apart,
God put different languages in everyone's heart.
This caused people to scatter, to seek a new land,
And to settle with those they could understand.

PATRIARCHS (2007B.C--1876B.C.)

Abraham

Three centuries later God was ready to start
His plan of redemption to heal man's sinful heart.
God chose Abram, a fatherless man,
And his barren wife, Sarai, to start His great Plan.
God singled him out as a man He could trust
To teach of God's ways, as a good father must.
God said, "Leave behind your land and relation,
And I'll make of you a powerful nation.
Your numbers will be too high to count,
Like the stars in the sky, a huge, vast amount.
Through you all families on Earth will be blest;
Through you I will give My very best.
Those who curse you will have trouble in store;
Those who bless you, I will bless evermore."
Abram told God that they were way past their prime,
But God promised a son would come in due time.

Lot

Nephew Lot went along but was an intrusion,
Which eventually caused no little confusion.
They set up camp between Bethel and Ai;

This was where Abram and Lot said good bye.
Their flocks and herds had grown so grand,
There simply was not enough grazing land.
It was time for their alliance to quit.
Each would keep is his own cattle, and they would split.
Lot chose a land that was fertile and fair.
He went east toward Sodom, and Abram stayed there.

The Covenant

Sodom was ransacked by four kings of renown;
They captured Lot and the whole town.
When Abram heard, he cut no slack.
He took his household of men and got everything back.
Then the high priest of Salem, in a meeting divine,
Blessed Abram and offered him bread and wine:
"Blessed are you, Abram, with this victory,
For God helped you to conquer your enemy."
Abram gave Priest Melchizedek a tenth of the spoil
And gave the rest to his men for their labor and toil.
God appeared to Abram by His holy Word
And repeated the promise he'd already heard:
"I'm giving this land to your descendants and you.
Now take a ram, goat, and heifer and cut them in two,"
For a covenant requires blood to be shed.
A sleep came on Abram that filled him with dread.
He dreamed four hundred years of slavery awaited,
Which would end in a victory to be celebrated.
Then Abram saw two fires pass through
The path of the animals which had been cut in two.
This was the covenant, the Old Testament's seal,
And Abram knew God's promise was real.

Ishmael

Sarai got nervous, and she jumped the gun;
She offered her servant to give Abram a son.
To the servant girl, Haggar, Ishmael was born.

Then she despised Sarai and held her in scorn.
Like a wild donkey, God said Ishmael would be
And live with his brothers in hostility.

A Divine Visitation

When Ishmael was thirteen and Abram ninety nine,
Abram had a visit from the Lord God divine.
He established with Abram deeper relations,
"Your name shall be Abraham, a 'father of nations'.
No longer Sarai shall her name be,
But now, Sarah, mother of My family.
I will give you the land of Canaan to possess;
It is Mine to give, and you're Mine to bless.
This promise is for the son of your wife;
You and Sarah shall soon bring forth a new life.
I will bless Ishmael because he is your relation,
And out of him, too, I will make a great nation.
Every male in your household must be circumcised;
By this will our covenant be recognized."
Abraham was exceedingly quick to obey,
And all males were circumcised that very day.
(And still today it's the sign in a man
That he is a descendant from Abraham's clan.)

Another Visitation

Three men came to visit Abraham one day;
The Lord and two angels were on their way
To destroy the towns of Gomorrah and Sodom,
For their morals had sunk to the absolute bottom.
Abraham invited the men for a meal.
When their meal ended, Abraham made an appeal,
"Would you spare Sodom if you find fifty good men?"
They said they would save it if there were just ten.
The Lord also brought a message of mirth,
"Next year at this time Sarah will give birth."

Sarah laughed when this was told,
"Shall I have this pleasure when I am so old?"

Sodom and Gomorrah Destroyed

Sodom was filled with severe moral rot;
The angels proceeded and found Nephew Lot.
They told Lot to leave with his family
And not to look back once they started to flee:
"For the stench of this place has confronted the Lord
And can no longer be allowed or ignored."
Fire and brimstone poured down from the sky;
For Sodom and Gomorrah this was good-bye.
Lot's wife looked back and turned into salt.
(Ignoring instructions can bring a deadly result.)

Isaac

God honored Abraham because he believed,
And at ninety years old, Sarah finally conceived.
Thus Isaac was born, a name which means laughter,
And more of Christ's lineage would soon follow after.
Ishmael and Haggar made fun of the child.
This, of course, drove Sarah wild,
So she said to Abraham, "They have to go."
And God told Abraham, "Yes, that is so.
The promise is through Isaac, your seed."
So Abraham gave them the supplies they would need.
But out in the desert they became thirsty and dry;
Then from Heaven, God heard Ishmael cry.
A well of water then came into view.
From the seed of Ishmael, the Arab nation grew.

Abraham Offers Isaac

Isaac, Abraham's son and his joy and prize,
God now required for a burnt sacrifice.
God called Abraham's name from above,

"Abraham, offer Me the son that you love."
So Abraham took Isaac up Moriah's great hill;
He was willing to allow his son's blood to spill.
He had no fear, so great was his faith,
That his son would return, even from death.
God made a Promise, and His Promise is true;
Isaac would simply have to come through.
With the wood on his back, Isaac carried the load
Like One many years later on Calvary's Road.
Isaac lay on the altar, trusting God for his life,
When God called out, "Abraham, put down your knife."
Then caught in the thicket, God provided a ram,
Showing only God can provide the Sacrifice Lamb.
Because of Abraham's obedience and all he had done,
God now was committed to offer His Son.
Abraham's seed, Isaac, was planted that day;
Christ would be the harvest--still years away.
(That's why God said, and today's still the same,
He's called Father Abraham when speaking his name.)

Isaac and Rebekah

When Abraham was old and Sarah was dead,
The time had now come for Isaac to wed.
Abraham sent his servant to his relative's land
To seek a virgin for Isaac and ask for her hand.
The servant prayed, "Lord, help me find Isaac's pearl;
If she waters my camels, let that be the girl."
As he was waiting at the watering site,
There came lovely Rebekah, to the servant's delight.
She graciously offered his camels some water.
Then he discovered she was a relative's daughter.
She invited him home, and the relatives knew
That this was God's plan--that the servant spoke true.
He took Rebekah to Canaan the very next day;
Isaac married Rebekah without any delay.

Jacob

Rebekah was barren, but Isaac believed;
He prayed to God and she finally conceived.
As Rebekah was growing and becoming full bloom,
God said, "Two nations are struggling inside your womb.
The descendants of one would surpass the other;
The older would serve the younger brother."
So Rebekah birthed twins, Jacob and Esau;
They were as opposite as the ends of a seesaw.
Esau was red and covered with hair;
Jacob was smooth with a complexion so fair.
Esau hunted and loved the outdoors;
Jacob liked home and helping with chores.
Esau, being born first, would be next in line
To receive the blessing and the Promise divine.
But he sold Jacob his birthright in exchange for a meal.
Then Jacob stole Esau's blessing, which was an ordeal:
Rebekah told Jacob, "We must be discreet."
Then she fixed for Isaac his favorite meat.
Jacob covered his arms with a skin of goat's hair.
Being blind, Isaac could not see who was there.
Jacob took Isaac the food, his special dish,
And said, "I am Esau and have done as you wish."
Isaac heard Jacob's voice but smelled Esau's clothes.
Convinced by the hair and the scent in his nose,
Isaac passed on the blessing to his second-born son.
When Esau came home, the deed had been done.
Esau was livid, and he had his fill.
He hated Jacob and vowed he would kill.
Rebekah knew she must diffuse this great strife,
So she suggested to Isaac that Jacob look for a wife.
Hopefully with Jacob no longer around,
Esau's anger toward Jacob would simmer down.
So Isaac sent Jacob to the land of his mother
To marry a daughter of Laban, Rebekah's brother.

Jacob's Ladder

Isaac blessed Jacob and sent him away.
At night Jacob found a good place to stay.
He set up camp and lay his head on a stone;
He dreamed of a stairway that led to God's throne.
Jacob saw angels moving in each direction.
At the top of the stairs the Lord stood in perfection,
Saying, "I give you this land, on which you are sleeping,
And to your descendants to be for their keeping. ✡
Your offspring will number as the dust of the ground;
Through you will all of Earth's blessing abound.
As I spoke to your fathers, I now speak to you;
You will have My protection. My promise is true.
You will return to this land of your destination."
In the morning Jacob continued toward his mother's relation.

Jacob Meets Rachel

When Jacob saw Cousin Rachel, it was love at first sight.
He worked seven years for her, all with delight.
Uncle Laban caused Jacob to live a victimized life;
When Jacob married, he took the wrong wife.
Leah sneaked in at the wedding to take Rachel's place;
To be an older, single sister was a public disgrace.
One week later Jacob in marriage took Rachel's hand
And worked seven more years at Laban's command.
But all of this, too, was part of God's Plan;
His wives and their maids birthed Israel's clan.
Leah was fertile and bore Jacob six sons.
Their maids, Bilhah and Zilpah, birthed four little ones.
At last Rachel conceived and gave birth to a son.
She named him Joseph, saying, "There's another to come."

Jacob Leaves Laban

Jacob finally told Laban, "My duty is done.
God has told me that it is time to move on."
For twenty years he was such a hard-working man

That Laban devised evil schemes to foil his plan.
Jacob realized that they'd have to flee,
So he secretly left with his family.
Laban wasn't about to cut any slack;
He went after Jacob to make them come back.
Their conflict at last came to a head,
But God had warned Laban to watch what he said.
Finally they agreed to leave each other alone,
And they sealed their pact with an altar of stone.
Jacob's dealings with Laban forever were done;
Then Laban went home, and Jacob moved on.

Wrestling with God

Jacob heard that his brother, Esau, was near.
Because he had tricked him, Jacob's heart filled with fear.
Jacob prayed, "O God of my grandfather and father,
Rescue me and my family from the hand of my brother.
You promised my descendants would be too high to count,
Like the sands of the seashore, an endless amount."
He sent his children and wives to hide out of sight;
Then a stranger came and wrestled Jacob that night.
He smote Jacob's hip and put it out of place.
Jacob didn't know he was fighting God face to face.
When Jacob realized Whom he was addressing,
He held on to the Lord and demanded a blessing.
The Lord asked Jacob, "What is your name?"
Since he had deceived Isaac, this was no game.
Jacob was truthful and answered Him well.
Then God changed his name to Israel.
His new name meant prince; a new life unveiled,
For he had wrestled with God, and he had prevailed.

Jacob Faces Esau

Jacob sent his servants ahead to give as a gift
Sheep and cattle to Esau to help mend the rift.
With four hundred men, Esau finally appeared.

This was the moment Jacob had feared.
Esau ran to his brother with a hearty embrace;
He hugged Jacob's neck and with tears kissed his face.
Esau asked, "Who are these women and children I see?"
"These are my family God has given to me."
Each one went forth, as one might expect,
And bowed to Esau to show him respect.
Esau tried to refuse the cattle and sheep,
But Jacob insisted, "They're a gift, yours to keep;
For I am relieved of this worrisome trial,
And the smile on your face is like seeing God smile."
Joseph watched his uncle extend mercy and grace;
One day he would find himself in the same place.
With the matter now settled in each brother's heart,
In peace the brothers were able to part.

Joseph (1920B.C.--1810B.C.)

Jealous Brothers

Again Rachel conceived as she had declared.
She died giving birth, but the baby was spared.
Jacob was thankful for baby Benjamin's life,
And with sorrow, near Bethlehem, Jacob buried his wife.
The first ten sons of Jacob were a jealous sight,
Especially of Joseph, his father's delight.
Jacob gave Joseph a beautiful coat;
He felt very important, and it was hard not to gloat.
At age seventeen Joseph had dreams
That prompted his brothers to devise terrible schemes.
He dreamed that his brothers would bow down one day--
Bow at his feet with homage to pay.
He dreamed that they were twelve sheaves of wheat,
And eleven sheaves bowed down at his feet.
Then they were stars in the galaxy;
Joseph said, "All of the stars bowed down to me."
Do you think when they heard this his brothers were glad?
They fussed, and they fumed and really were mad!

The brothers wanted him gone, and to accomplish their goal,
They threw poor, young Joseph into a hole.
When a caravan of traders came into view,
Judah said, "Murder is something we must not do,"
So the brothers sold Joseph for a fair price;
The traders took him to Egypt as their merchandise.
The brothers showed Jacob his son's bloody coat,
Not telling they'd rubbed it with the blood of a goat.
Jacob was completely undone,
"A beast must have killed my dear, precious son."

Joseph in Egypt

Potiphar was captain of Pharaoh's guard;
He was well respected and worked very hard.
Joseph was sold to become Potiphar's slave;
He did such a fine job, his master would rave.
Everything flourished under Joseph's wise hand,
So over his household he was put in command.
He was Potiphar's favorite, a slave he could trust,
But Potiphar's wife was a woman of lust.
She tried to tempt Joseph; she was worse than a flirt.
Joseph ran away quickly, but she grabbed his shirt.
Then she accused Joseph, and his shirt was the proof.
When Potiphar heard this, he raised the roof.
Godly, good Joseph was falsely accused
And locked up in prison, which God clearly used.
The prison keeper, seeing that Joseph was bright,
Made Joseph the prefect to help things run right.
Joseph interpreted some dreams in the prison;
A butler and baker heard truth through his vision.
The baker was hanged, and the butler went free;
It happened just as Joseph said it would be.

One night Pharaoh had dreams, and he had a fit.
His wizards couldn't help him one little bit.
Pharaoh despaired, "Who can help me, who can?"

The butler spoke up, "I know just the man.
He interpreted dreams for the baker and me,
And things happened just as he said they would be."
So at age thirty Joseph walked out of his cell;
His future achievements are something to tell.
Having been called at Pharaoh's command,
Joseph was brought before Pharaoh to stand.
"I've had some dreams, but I don't have a clue."
Joseph answered, "My God will give the meaning to you."
Joseph humbly listened to Pharaoh so great.
As he told Joseph his dream, he began to relate:
"There were seven fat cows in a field so green;
Then came seven more that were skinny and lean.
The skinny cows ate the ones who were fat;
Tell me please, Joseph, the meaning of that.
I then saw seven sheaves of wheat in a field;
They were abundant and gave a large yield.
Seven scrawny sheaves then devoured them all,
But they still stayed scrawny, withered and small."
Joseph interpreted without hesitation;
His wisdom and counsel would save the great nation.
Joseph told Pharaoh, "There will be a feast;
For seven years crops will be increased.
The next seven years will be hungry and poor,
But all can survive if food is in store.
You need a man who will know what to do."
Pharaoh told Joseph, "That man is you."
Pharaoh made Joseph number two in the nation;
And through this, Joseph became his brothers' salvation.

The Famine

For seven years the crops were so many;
Then all of a sudden, there just were not any.
But Egypt had plenty, enough for the drought.
This news traveled to Canaan, and Joseph's family found out.
The famine was worse than his brothers had thought,

So the ten journeyed to Egypt where food could be bought.
They met with Joseph, but they didn't know
That he was their brother till he told them so.
Joseph accused his brothers of spying;
He asked them questions and said they were lying.
All of this time his brothers were scared.
They tried to tell Joseph why they should be spared.
They explained they had a father and brother
And even mentioned they'd once had another.
They remembered their Joseph only too well
And regretted they ever decided to sell.
For three days Joseph put the brothers in prison
Then released only nine, but kept Brother Simeon.
Joseph gave them grain and sent them away;
Into their sacks he sneaked all their pay.
He told them he would never see them again
Unless they brought their young brother Ben.

Once again the food in Canaan was done,
But Jacob did not want to let go of his son.
Benjamin, born to Rachel, was all he had left,
And since the loss of Joseph, he felt so bereft.
"We can't go without Ben; if we stay, we will die."
So Jacob gave his permission and waved them good-bye.
When they got to Egypt, they were ready to deal,
But Joseph invited them in for a meal.
They were seated in the birth rank of each other;
Benjamin was given more food than any brother.
The brothers wondered at this strange event.
Then they got some grain, and homeward they went.
The steward chased after, saying, "Give yourselves up!
My master is missing his silver cup."
"Why would we return such kindness with malice?"
But in Benjamin's sack, he found Joseph's chalice.
This was a test that Joseph had planned,
For the cup had been placed there at his command.

The brothers cried out, "This can't be true!
Stealing is something he never would do."
They went back to Joseph; then Judah pled,
"Don't punish Benjamin; take me instead.
If we go home without this young lad,
It would bring death to our gray-headed dad.
He is the only son left from his mother;
I offer my life on behalf of this brother."
This was all Joseph needed to know;
He started crying and told his servants to go.
"I am Joseph your brother, the one that you sold;
God has fulfilled all that He foretold.
It all has happened as He planned it would;
What you meant for evil, God meant for good."

The reunion of brothers was both bitter and sweet,
And Joseph forgave them as they bowed at his feet.
Joseph now understood, and he was so glad
That God used him to save his brothers and dad.

The Move to Egypt

Joseph's father, his brothers, all of their wives,
And all of their children totaled seventy lives.
They all moved to Egypt because of Joseph's high seat;
They received their own land and had plenty to eat.
When Jacob saw Joseph, he let out a cry,
"My Joseph's alive! Now in peace I can die."
Jacob's twelve sons became the twelve Tribes.
From Judah, the fourth son, as the Bible describes,
Would issue God's Gift of a Savior and King,
(The One at whose birth the angels would sing.)

Before Joseph died at one hundred and ten,
He said, "You will return to Canaan again.
When you leave Egypt, take my bones too."
The Israelites promised that's what they would do.

MOSES (1526B.C.--1406B.C.)

This move to Egypt at first was so great,
But it gradually affected all of Israel's fate.
After these brothers had gone to their graves,
All their descendants became Egypt's slaves.
In four hundred years the Israelites grew,
And about two million made up their slave crew.
The Egyptians were nervous as their numbers did soar.
Would these people rebel and with Egypt make war?
So Pharaoh devised a horrible plan:
They would kill each baby boy to get rid of the man.

It was at this time Jochebed gave birth
To one whom God called the "humblest on earth."
Baby Moses was put in a basket of reeds
And hidden in the Nile, concealed by weeds.
There Pharaoh's daughter heard the wee baby groan;
She discovered the babe and made him her own.
Miriam was secretly watching her baby brother
And offered a wet nurse, the baby's own mother.
Moses' mother was hired to nurse her own son;
She taught him God's Promise and the things to be done.

Moses grew up in the palace in great luxury,
But he ached for his people and wanted them free.
When Moses was a strong, caring young man,
He saw an Egyptian beating one of his clan.
Angered, he left the Egyptian for dead,
And because he'd been seen, to the desert he fled.

Moses journeyed to Midian and sat by a well;
Jethro's seven daughters came from the dell.
They came to fetch water to fill up their trough,
But some shepherds came and chased the girls off.
So Moses stepped up and helped the girls deal.
Jethro said, "Invite this good man for a meal."

Moses was glad for the kind invitation.
Jethro's home became his habitation.
In marriage Moses took daughter Zipporah's hand;
He now had a new family in a new land.
For forty years Moses led a peaceable life,
Shepherding and raising two sons with his wife.

The Burning Bush

One day as Moses was tending the flock,
Something happened that made his world rock.
On the mountainside a burning bush loomed;
Although it was burning, it was not consumed.
As Moses checked out this unusual sight,
A voice spoke from the bush with power and might.
The voice called, "Moses," as he looked around,
"Take off your shoes; this is holy ground.
I'm the God of your fathers, and I've heard the plea
Of the Israelite slaves who are crying to Me.
I now come down to break Pharaoh's hand
And to deliver My people into their own land."
The voice continued, as the bush kept on burning,
"Go now to Egypt, it's time for returning--
To rescue my people and set them all free."
"But why," Moses asked, "should they listen to me?"
"Say that I AM THAT I AM has sent you their way,
And they are to follow, to trust and obey."
(Jesus says that He is I AM in John, chapter eight,
But people can't receive this message so great.)
Then God told Moses to cast down his rod;
Moses needed to see the power of God.
Moses' rod quickly turned into a snake;
Moses jumped back and started to quake.
God said, "Now pick up the snake by its tail."
It turned back to a rod as hard as a rail.
Again Moses continued to balk,

"I'm slow of speech, and I cannot talk."
God assured Moses He would be there to guide
And that his brother, Aaron, would be by his side.

Moses conferred with Jethro about God's assignment.
Jethro agreed, and they came into alignment.
God had spoken, and there was no doubt,
So with his wife and two sons, Moses set out.
Aaron greeted Moses as he entered the land,
For God had told Aaron about His command.
They spoke to the elders of the Israelite crew,
So they would know what God planned to do.
They were relieved and all in accord;
They gave thanks to God and worshiped the Lord.

The Exodus

Moses and Aaron went to speak to the Pharaoh.
He was hard-hearted, and his mind was so narrow.
Moses said, "Let my people go to worship our God,
Or many great plagues will come on your sod.
We need a three days journey to worship the Lord,
Lest He fall upon us with pestilence or sword."
Pharaoh said, "No, who's your God anyway?
You are our slaves, and you have to obey."
After this, Pharaoh's demands became worse.
The Israelites blamed Moses for bringing a curse.
But God assured Moses this was the hour
To free the slaves and show His mighty power.

Then came the plagues of frogs, boils, and flies,
Darkness, death, and hail from the skies.
The water in the Nile turned into blood;
Locusts ate all the crops, leaving fields of mud.
Through nine dreadful plagues the Pharaoh'd not bend,
So the tenth final plague God had to send.

The Israelites put a lamb's blood over the door,
So when the Angel of Death came, he would pass o'er.
But the Egyptians didn't know this could be done,
And so in each family died the very first son.
(Thus we escape death through the blood of the Lamb,
When we accept Jesus, the great God, I AM.)
After this, the Pharaoh finally told them to go;
God said to prepare so they would not be slow:
"Dress for a long journey to a new land.
Lace up your sandals; have your staff in your hand."
God touched the Egyptians so out they doled
Gifts to the Israelites of silver and gold--
And also supplies of things they would need.
They packed Joseph's bones and left with "God's speed".
They took herds of cattle and flocks of sheep
And trusted that God would tend to their keep.

Soon the Israelites started to cry,
"Moses, did you bring us here so we could die?"
They journeyed until they came to the Red Sea;
Moses lifted his rod and said, "Follow me."
Then came a wind with such power and force,
They knew that God was directing their course.
The water rolled back, and they passed safely through,
But the Egyptian Army was out to pursue.
They followed the Israelites through the path in the sea,
But the water closed in, and they could not flee.

The Passover

Then God spoke to Moses, "You must celebrate
Your deliverance from Egypt on this very date.
These miracles that I have performed for your nation
Must always be taught to each generation.
Now you shall enter the land of the Canaanites,

The Hitites, Hivites, Amorites, and Jebusites.
The land I will give you (better than money)
Will be a land flowing with milk and with honey."

The Ten Commandments

They lived as nomads in the wilderness land
As they were learning to trust God's guiding hand.
Now the Spirit of God led Moses aright
With a cloud in the day and by fire at night.
To this humble servant and leader of men
God gave the Commandments, numbering ten.
God told Moses to climb Mount Sinai alone;
There God gave him The Law written in stone.
The Commandments are simple and very direct,
And we will be blessed if we give them respect:
"Honor God first, love, and obey.
Remember Him weekly on His Sabbath day.
You shall not practice idolatry.
You shall not commit adultery.
You shall not be careless in using God's name;
He will not hold you guiltless if you use it in vain.
You shall not lie, steal, or murder another.
You shall honor your father and honor your mother.
You shall not covet a man's goods or his wife."
If you keep these commands, you will live a blessed life.
(These wonderful laws, written in stone,
Show that our lives are sacred and all that we own.)

People have struggled right from the beginning;
The Commandments showed men that they were sinning.
These laws found mankind in a bad situation,
For the practice of sin brings ruination.
These laws were not given to destroy man's fun
But to lead to the Savior, the Compassionate One.

The Priesthood

Moses was a descendant of Jacob's son Levi.
Brother Aaron was anointed high priest of the bevy.
Exodus describes the priests' garb to the hilt
And especially how the Lord's tent was built.
The gold they received, when God broke their shackle,
Was given for use in the tabernacle.
Only Levi's descendants were allowed to be priests
To serve the Lord in all worship and feasts.
The book of *Leviticus* describes in detail
How offerings were made every day without fail.
The blood of cattle and sheep was outpoured
To cover their sins and make peace with the Lord.

The Forty-Year Delay

After two years under Moses' command,
God told them to enter the Promised Land.
So twelve spies went to Canaan to gather a view;
All returned frightened, all except two.
They were Caleb and Joshua who said, "Let us enter in;
Although they are giants, with God we will win."
But the people were frightened, and with wild raves,
They said, "Let us go back and become Egypt's slaves!"
God was so angry because He had led them;
He had protected, clothed them, and fed them.
God sent food called manna, which formed on the ground,
And every morning there was enough to go 'round.
Out of a rock, water abundantly poured;
All of their needs had been met by the Lord.
God said, "Because of rebellion you will not enter in;
You will die in the wilderness, so great is your sin.
For forty years you will wander about,
Till those twenty and older have completely died out."

Moses Disobeys

The Lord moved them to Zin with no water in sight.
The people blamed Moses and were ready to fight.
God told Moses, "Gather the people around
And speak to the rock that lies on the ground.
My people must learn not to grumble and pout.
When you speak to the rock, I'll pour water out.
The Israelites must learn of My holiness,
That I am their Rock and I want to bless."
Moses scolded the people, "You rebellious flock!"
Then two times in anger he struck the rock.
Water gushed out in abundant supply.
God said, "Moses, because you did not comply
And did not trust Me to do as I planed,
You will not enter the Promised Land."

Moses Farewell

Forty years of wandering finally had past;
The Israelites were ready to move on at last.
During this time they practiced God's word
And learned from the things they'd seen and heard.
They now had a Godly identity
And had lost their slavery mentality.
Before ascending Mount Nebo on his final walk,
Moses spoke to his listening flock:
"Everyone must wisely choose his direction.
If you choose God, you will have His protection.
If you rebel and go your own way,
You'll find there is a high price to pay.
Though you are scattered to the ends of the earth,
God will bring you back to the land of your birth." ✡
After Moses finished his marvelous talk,
He ascended the mountain for his heaven-bound walk.
At one hundred and twenty years old
Moses viewed the land that God had foretold.

Then God's humble servant breathed his last breath,
Still strong and healthy right up to his death.
God buried his body and took him to glory.
Through Moses God tells His deliverance story.

THE PROMISED LAND

Jericho, Rahab and Achan

The Lord chose Joshua, Moses' right hand,
To lead His people and be in command.
Joshua sent two spies forth to scout,
But the King of Jericho was soon to find out.
A harlot, named Rahab, had a house on the wall.
It was to her that the spies made a call.
The King's messengers went to capture the spies,
But Rahab was quick to protect them with lies:
"Who these men are, they didn't say,
But they left at dusk and are now on their way.
The spies should not be far out of sight."
So the king's men pursued them that very night.
Rahab went to her roof and got the spies out of hiding.
She knew that on them her future was riding:
"The people of Jericho know of your goal,
And the fear of your God has captured our soul.
Now that I've spared you and am setting you free,
I ask your protection for my family and me."
The spies said to Rehab, "You have a deal.
We will protect because you didn't squeal."
Rahab and the spies gave each other hope.
The spies left through her window by a red rope,
Saying, "When we attack, hang this rope from your wall,
So we can protect you, and you will not fall."
The Jews kept Rahab and her family safe and alive.
She became David's great-great grandmother: Matthew one: five.

The Lord, Israel's Commander-in-Chief,
Gave to Joshua this strategy brief:

"Your army must march around Jericho,
One time around for six days in a row.
As you march do not make a sound.
On day seven march seven times 'round.
Then blow your horns and give a loud shout.
Don't be afraid; don't even doubt.
The wall will collapse before your very eyes;
Save Rahab's household for hiding the spies.
Since Jericho is your first victory,
Let the silver and gold be an offering to Me."
Jericho's destruction was thorough and grand,
And Joshua's name brought fear to the land.

After Jericho, Joshua sent some men out to spy
On a small Amorite town known as Ai.
They said, "Three thousand men can get the job done."
But soon little Ai had them on the run.
Joshua and the leaders, with their heads in the dust,
Cried, "Where is the God we thought we could trust?"
God said, "Get up! Get your face off the ground.
There is sin in the camp, and it must be found."
So each tribe came forward, then each separate clan,
And the Lord pointed out the one guilty man.
From the tribe of Judah, a man, Achan by name,
Caused Israel's defeat, and he was to blame.
Joshua said to Achan, "Give God the glory;
Now you must confess and tell the true story."
Achan said, "When I saw the silver and bar of pure gold,
I wanted to have it, along with a robe.
I buried them all under my tent."
Then to dig up the goods, a few men were sent.
They found the goods, as per Achan's confession.
He and his family were stoned for his transgression.
(The consequences of sin always are strong.
A whole nation can suffer when someone does wrong.)
After Israel's shameful defeat,
With the sin removed, Ai was easy to beat.

God Stops the Sun

Five Amorite kings led an attack
Against the Gibeonites who couldn't fight back.
So the Israelites quickly came to their aid,
All because of a peace pact they had made.
When the Amorites were almost defeated,
More time was all that Joshua needed.
It was this battle of Gibeon where Joshua prayed,
"Lord, hold back the sun." And back the sun stayed.
Never has there been a day like that one,
Where by human request the Lord stopped the sun.
The Israelites thrived under Joshua's command;
They conquered thirty one kings to enter their land.

Judges **(1350B.C.--1050B.C.)**

Now at last the Israelites had their own land,
And God chose judges to be in command.
But the Israelites turned their back on the Lord.
They were a selfish and Baal-worshiping hoard.
So the Lord allowed them to fall into defeat;
Then they repented, but their mistakes they'd repeat.
(When the people had troubles, they sought God to blame,
But people need changing, for God's always the same.)

Deborah

During this strife and struggle and all,
God had His judges who heeded His call.
Through Deborah God performed a marvelous feat;
They conquered the Canaanites with a victory complete.

Gideon

But the Israelites again fell into sin,
And the Midianites moved right on in.
The Israelites fled to the hills, hiding in caves,
And cried out to Yahweh, the true God who saves.

God heard their call and chose a man, Gideon,
To be the one who would free them from Midian.
While Gideon was hiding to stay out of sight,
God came to him saying, "O man of great might,
You are My man; the Lord is with thee,
For I will lead you to great victory.
I want you to lead your people in war,
So the Midianites can oppress you no more."
Gideon protested, "Lord, You've got the wrong man;
I'm the least in my family from the lowliest clan."
God persuaded Gideon to take on this great task.
Before the battle, Gideon had a favor to ask.
Gideon asked, "Lord, let me put out a fleece."
God kindly agreed so he could have peace.
"Let me put a lamb's fleece out on the lawn;
Let it be filled with water by dawn,
But the grass around will still be bone dry."
And it was so, for God did comply.
Gideon asked for a next time around,
"This time when I put the fleece on the ground,
The grass will be wet, but the fleece will be dry."
And that's how it happened; God again did comply.

God diminished the army to only three hundred;
The Israelites were completely out numbered.
Gideon divided the group into three
And surrounded the camp of the enemy.
In the stillness of night, it happened so fast;
They blew on their horns with a frightening blast.
They smashed jars and pots made of clay
And waved their torches, starting the fray.
In confusion the Midianites were quickly undone;
The enemy scattered, and the Israelites won.
Gideon was no longer controlled by his fears.
After this, Gideon ruled a full forty years.

Samson

Again Israel rebelled and fell into sinning,
But God had His man right from the beginning.
His name was Samson, who had God's special strength,
Who vowed not to drink wine and keep his hair natural length.
Samson became the Philistines' Enemy-One,
For it seems Samson always had them on the run.
Then to Delilah, God's man lost his heart.
In dealing with Samson, she played a great part.
She was a Philistine, and they needed her aid.
If she found Samson's secret, she would be paid.
The Philistine leaders would each pay a great price.
Delilah did not have to think twice.
Three times Samson told her, but really he lied,
And when the Philistines seized him, he pushed them aside.
Delilah cried, "You don't love me, now I look like a fool.
Tell me your secret, and don't be so cruel."
So he told her his secret of why he was strong;
It was because of his vow to keep his hair long.
Then she lulled him to sleep, and as swift as a fox,
And a man came in and shaved off his locks.
Then she awoke Samson and amidst all the cries,
The Philistines grabbed him and put out his eyes.
They took him to prison, bound with a chain,
Where he worked like an ox, grinding the grain.
God forgave Samson, and his strength slowly returned,
And for revenge Samson continually burned.

The Philistines were evil, and their gods were all pagan.
One day they assembled at the temple of Dagon
To celebrate their victory and Samson's defeat,
And to poke fun of Samson would make it complete.
They led Samson in and were having a ball;
Samson pushed on a pillar and caused it to fall.
Three thousand were killed in that very hour,
And Samson died too, but he died in God's power.

Samuel

A woman named Hannah felt sorrow and doom
Because the Lord had closed up her womb.
She went to the temple almost every day;
She would cry out to God, beseech Him and pray.
Priest Eli thought she was drunk and held her in disgust,
But then she explained, and she won his trust.
"I'll give my child to God if He gives me a son."
Eli blessed her and said, "It shall be done."
Thus Samuel was born, and as a young boy,
Hannah took him to Eli to be in his employ.
Young Samuel grew strong and heeded God's call;
Wise Samuel became the last judge of all.
The last verse in *Judges* explains Israel's demise:
"They did what was right in their own eyes."
(When man sets his own rules, there's no limit how low
Those who disregard God are able to go.)

KINGS (1050B.C.--586B.C.)

Samuel grew old and the future looked bad;
Israel wanted a king like other tribes had.
God told Samuel to warn: "With a king in command,
He'll enslave your offspring and take the best land.
He will tax your belongings for his support
And distribute your harvest to his people in court.
He'll take the best of your sheep and best of your cattle."
But they wanted a king who would lead them in battle.
Although Judge Samuel was very distraught,
God consented to give the king that they sought.

Saul

God told Samuel to anoint a man strong and tall;
God gave the people their choice when He picked King Saul.
God, willing to bless Saul, gave him His Spirit,
But Saul wanted to do things for his own merit.

He wanted to do things only his way,
And he would not listen to what God had to say.
Samuel advised Saul telling him what to do,
But Saul simply did not follow through.
So the Holy Spirit from Saul did depart,
And God chose another, one "after His heart".

David

God told Samuel to anoint a new man,
One who loves God and will follow His Plan.
Samuel traveled to Bethlehem, filling many with fear.
The people asked Samuel, "Why are you here?"
Samuel said, "I have a message to bring;
I'm to anoint Jesse's son to be the next king.
For by God, King Saul has been rejected;
I am here to anoint the one He's selected."
So Jesse brought forth his seven strong sons;
They all looked good but were not the right ones.
Samuel asked, "Do you not have another?"
"Yes, there is David, our youngest brother.
He's just a shepherd and carries a sling."
They couldn't imagine that he'd ever be king.
When Samuel saw David, he instantly knew;
He could tell by his face that his heart was true.
Samuel poured a horn of oil on David's head;
The Holy Spirit left Saul and filled David instead.

David and Goliath

David was a ruddy young lad.
He was given a chore by Jesse, his dad,
To take food to his brothers at the battle site,
Where the Israelites and Philistines were positioned to fight.
David checked out his brothers, delivered the food,
And found the Israelite army in a trembling mood.
He wasn't there long when he found out why;
That's when giant Goliath let out a cry:

"Give me a man from the army of Saul.
If he kills me, the victory goes to you all.
But if he dies, then our slaves you will be.
We'll settle this war with just him and me."
David cried in dismay as the Israelites fled,
"Who is this heathen who fills you with dread,
This uncircumcised one who is our foe?"
He stood almost ten feet from his head to his toe.
David's brother, Eliab, gave a belittling laugh,
"Who are you? Just a shepherd boy with a staff!"
David ran to King Saul, saying, "You must not fear;
I've killed a lion, and I've killed a bear!
Just give me a chance." King Saul agreed
And offered David his armor, which he didn't need.

David chose five smooth stones from the brook;
The stones and his sling were all that he took.
Goliath cursed David because of his youth.
David responded, shouting this truth:
"You come to me with a spear and a sword,
But I come to you in the name of the Lord.
I will smite you and cut off your head.
Wild animals will feast on all of your dead."
David then took a stone and slung it around.
The stone hit his brow, and Goliath fell to the ground.
With the giant's own sword, David cut off his head;
This time it was the Philistine army that fled.

David and King Saul

David now was a hero, more than the king.
Saul suffered depression and asked David to sing.
So David spent much time at the palace,
But Saul's love for David soon turned to malice.
Jealousy drove him to want David dead,
And for years from King Saul, David skillfully fled.
David vowed that he would never harm Saul,

For he was the king, and David honored his call.
The Philistines killed Saul and his three sons in the end,
Including Jonathan, David's dear friend.
Saul was pierced by an arrow; his body was gored.
He ended his life, falling on his own sword.

The people loved David and gathered around,
And as king of Judah, David was crowned.
For the House of King Saul, things did not go well,
And eventually David became king over all Israel.

David Conquers Jerusalem

David conquered Jerusalem and the fortress of Zion,
The future dwelling of the Christ, Judah's Lion.
David was given a palace by King Hiram of Tyre;
Now to build God a temple was David's desire,
"I have a large palace of fine cedar board
But only a tent for the ark of the Lord."
Touched by David's heart with a passion so true,
God told David what He wanted to do:
"I have journeyed with you; you were never alone,
But here I will dwell and establish your throne."
God then made a promise that nothing could sever:
"A Descendant of David will rule here forever.
I'll be his Father, and he'll be My Son."
Then David responded, "Let Your will be done."

Christ Prophesied in Psalms

In *Psalms* David pours out his heart with emotion,
Displaying his trust and perfect devotion:
"I bless you, O Lord, right from within,
For You heal our disease and forgive all our sin.
You protect those who call on Your name,
But the ungodly will be put to shame."

If we look closely in *Psalms*, Jesus we'll see,
God the Son, the Creator, our Deity.
We see that God's Son would come as a man,
And to suffer and die would be part of The Plan.
He would be betrayed by someone He knew,
And His hands and feet would be pierced cleanly through.
We see His bones out of place, but not one of them broken;
They would bid for His clothes by tossing a token.
He would be given vinegar because of His thirst
And feel abandoned by God before His heart burst.
We see the Messiah delivered from Hell
And ascending to Heaven with His Father to dwell.
One day there will be a revolt against God;
Then the Messiah will rule with His iron rod.
The Lord has made Zion His forever home,
Where David's descendant will sit on the throne.
In Matthew ten, two men deliver loud cries,
"Have mercy, Son of David, and heal our eyes."
For through King David, Jesus was royal at birth.
One day from this throne He'll rule the Earth.

David and Bathsheba

In battles of war David was a great winner,
And in moments of weakness he could be a great sinner.
He seduced Bathsheba, another man's wife,
And then plotted to take her husband's life.
Nathan the prophet said, "What have you done?
You know that you are the guilty one.
You have murdered Uriah and stolen his wife.
Now your household will suffer great strife."
When David heard this, he fell apart.
In *Psalm* fifty-one he poured out his heart.
He confessed his sin to the merciful Lord,
And by God's Holy Spirit, he was restored.

Bathsheba, being pregnant with a new life,
Moved to the palace and became David's wife.
The baby was born very sickly and weak;
David fervently prayed with words humble and meek.
Face down on he ground, he fasted and cried;
At seven days old, his baby boy died.
David freshened himself with vigor and vim,
Saying, "Though he can't return, one day I'll go to him."
David tended his wife as she tearfully grieved;
The Lord blessed Bathsheba, and she conceived.
The birth of Solomon brought joy in their pain,
A child favored by God who one day would reign.

The Census, the Threshingfloor and the Temple

Israel's large numbers filled David with pride.
David said, "Take a census of how many abide."
Joab, David's captain, warned this would be a sin,
Which David ignored and said, "Let the census begin."
When the census was over, God's anger was kindled,
So God sent a plague, and the numbers were dwindled.
The Lord told David's prophet how to settle the score,
"Build an altar to God on Ornan's threshingfloor."
David hastened to Ornan, a Jebusite,
To purchase his land to help end the plight.
Ornan said, "I give you this place and the oxen for free."
David said, "I can't give to the Lord if it doesn't cost me."
So he then paid Ornan a price that was right;
This place would become the Lord's temple site.
David built an altar, and God answered by fire.
Now to build God's temple became David's desire,
So David acquired building materials galore.
Then God said, "David, you've been a great man of war.
Solomon one day will rule in peace;
Let him build the temple, and let your work cease."

Solomon

Before David died, he prayed a powerful prayer,
Commending the kingdom to Solomon's care.
Solomon was great before God's loving eyes,
For he asked not for wealth, but just to be wise.
God faithfully granted Solomon's request;
Then with wealth and fame, he was abundantly blessed.
With David's provisions of silver and gold,
Solomon built the temple as he had been told.
When the temple was finished, there was great celebration;
The people all gathered for its dedication.
As their praises and prayers were being outpoured,
The glory of God filled the House of the Lord.
Then Solomon stood with his hands in the air
And proceeded to pray this significant prayer:
"All blessings come from You, God, in heaven.
When we sin and repent, may we be forgiven.
Let Your people be guided by Your decree
To punish the guilty and set the innocent set free.
When the land and crops become damaged or dry,
Show them Your way when You hear their cry.
When foreigners come because You dwell here,
May they come to know You as You answer their prayer.
If Israel is conquered because her sin,
May your people repent and turn to You once again.
If they are exiled under Your Righteous Hand,
Forgive and return them to their ancestors' land." ✡

Cutting the Baby in Two

There were two mothers with their babies in bed.
One mother awoke to find her baby dead.
So she switched the babies and took the live one,
Giving the sleeping mother her little, dead son.
When the mother awoke, she instantly knew
It wasn't her baby, and a big conflict grew.

One mother spoke true; the other spoke lies.
They went to King Solomon, who was ever so wise:
"If you can't agree, cut the baby in two;
One half goes to her and the other to you."
The true mother cried and spoke with alarm,
"Give the baby to her, and do him no harm."
The false mother said, "Divide the child in two."
King Solomon spoke, for he instantly knew,
"Give this one the baby; she's the mother thereof,
For she pled for her child with a true mother's love."

Proverbs

In *Proverbs* Solomon teaches many a truth,
So we can behave and not act uncouth:
"Knowing God's word is our greatest wealth;
It brings success and adds to our health.
The fool is one who rejects God in his heart;
He can never be wise but thinks he's so smart.
Every word that we speak with our breath
Carries the power of life or of death."
Solomon says to consider the ant;
You'll never hear him saying, "I can't."
"Don't hang with people who devise evil schemes;
That's one sure way to destroy your dreams.
Angry people, who are quickly annoyed,
Are the very people it is wise to avoid.
Men are fools who succumb to seduction;
They are playing a game that leads to destruction.
A man who is prideful and even aloof
Will only hate you if you give him reproof.
Have a cheerful heart, and don't be a nagger;
Never be lazy, and don't be a lagger.
God hates dishonesty right to His core;
Don't tip the scales so you can get more.
Do not co-sign another person's loan;
You'll lose your bed and all that you own.

The poor will never cease to be in the land;
God blesses those who give them a hand.
The commands are the lamp, and God's law is the light;
Through them a man can know wrong from right.
Sin always brings reproach to a nation;
When the guilty go free, it brings ruination.
More precious than rubies is a virtuous wife;
Her husband can trust her as she enriches his life."

The Book of *Proverbs* should be carefully studied;
It will clear the waters which have become muddied.
Although Solomon was a wonderful teacher,
He summed it all up in *Ecclesiastes, The Preacher:*
"The world's praise and wealth are just a vain thing;
Obeying the Lord is the only main thing."

Solomon's Demise

Although Solomon's teachings are true to this day,
He ignored God's wisdom and went very astray.
Throughout his kingship he made bad decisions,
And his disobedience caused many divisions.
Solomon married many wives from lands far away
And built idols for them at which they could pray.
God said, "Because you have an idolatrous heart,
I will take your nation and tear it apart.
But because of your father, David, this won't be done
Until the kingdom goes to Rehoboam, your son."

The Nation Divided

When the day came that Solomon died,
Rehoboam became king, a man filled with pride.
He threatened to rule with unbending force,
Which put the nation on a whole different course.
The ten tribes of Israel chose a new head;
From Rehoboam's kingship they willfully fled.
And so the land was divided, and when all was through,

There were ten tribes called Israel, and Judah had two.
Jeroboam became king of Israel's ten tribes.
He was known for evil and as a man who gave bribes.
God said, "I will build you a strong dynasty
If you follow My laws and listen to Me."
But Jeroboam threw all that away
And built two golden calves to which people could pray.
The ten tribes of Israel dwelt in the north,
And from the southern land Judah, Jesus came forth.
All the kings in Israel were filled with evil and hate,
But in Judah some kings were evil, and some kings were great.

PROPHETS (855B.C--433B.C.)

Because most of the kings did not have God's heart,
It is now that the prophets play a big part.

Elijah

Elijah Stops the Rain

Israel's King Ahab caused struggle and strife,
Making all worship Baal with Jezebel his wife.
God's prophet, Elijah, who was from Gilead,
Was bidden by God to speak to Ahab.
So Elijah went to King Ahab, looking absurd,
Saying, "There will be no more rain till I give the word.
Surely as before the Lord God I stand,
I've delivered this message at His command."
Then God told Elijah to go quickly and hide
Where ravens would feed him by the riverside.
It came to pass, with no rain from the sky,
The brook, named Cherith, became totally dry.

The Widow of Zarephath

God said, "There's a widow getting ready to die
Because she's at the end of her scanty supply."
So to this widow in Zarephath, Elijah fled.

This is how they were miraculously fed:
The widow and her son were on their last bite
When Prophet Elijah came into sight.
He asked for some water and her last cake;
With a handful of flour, that was all she could make.
Elijah said, "Don't be afraid to make it for me;
There'll be plenty for thy son and for thee."
From that time on, even in drought,
Her flour and oil never ran out.
During this time, the widow's son died.
To Elijah the widow mournfully cried,
"Did God take my son because I didn't obey?"
Elijah then took her son and started to pray.
With the boy on his bed, Elijah lay on his form;
After praying three times, the boy became warm.

The Contest between God and Baal

When the drought was in the third year,
God told Elijah to reappear
Before King Ahab, where he made an appeal.
King Ahab was desperate and ready to deal.
Elijah told Ahab there must be a test,
So the people could see which god is the best.
Elijah challenged four hundred fifty prophets of Baal,
And they would all die if their god should fail.
About this contest it was agreed,
If the Lord God should win, all would concede.
The contest was simple, and the rules were good;
They would meet on Mount Carmel with two bundles of wood.
With the wood and two bulls they would each build a pyre,
And only their god could set it on fire.

Baal's prophets implored Baal from morning till three.
Elijah just laughed and teased them with glee.
Then Elijah went to his pyre and watered it good;

He watered the stones, the bull and the wood.
Then unto the Lord, Elijah gave out a call;
Fire shot down from heaven, consuming bull, stones, and all.
After this, all of Baal's prophets were slain,
And God completed the victory by sending the rain.

Elisha

When the victory was over, Elijah felt so bereft
That he cried out to God, "I'm the only one left."
God answered Elijah, "There's no reason to wail;
There are yet seven thousand who have not bowed to Baal."
God told Elijah to cast off his gloom:
"Thou shall anoint Elisha to take over thy room."
For Elijah this really lifted the load,
And he left his cave and went down the road.
Elijah found young Elisha plowing his field;
Elijah tossed him his cloak, and their connection was sealed.
Elisha said his good-byes and left with his friend
To serve his new master to the glorious end.
Elisha very closely to Elijah did cleave.
He asked for double his power if Elijah should leave.
Elijah said to Elisha, "If you see as I go,
You'll have double-power, and that's how you'll know."
A chariot of fire swooped down from the sky,
And a whirlwind took Elijah to Heaven so high.
Elisha watched as his friend faded from view,
Then took off his robe and tore it in two.
He took Elijah's cloak, being very excited,
And struck the Jordan, and the river divided.
Elisha's ministry was both humble and grand,
For he did mighty things for the folks in the land.

Jars of Oil

There was a young widow who had a great debt;
She had no money for her needs to be met.
She went to Elisha and asked him what to do.

He said, "Get lots of jars, not just a few.
Take all of your jars, and then borrow some more;
Go to your home, and then shut your door.
Pour the oil you have into each jar,
And God will increase it and make it go far."
From one small jar of oil, the quantity grew;
The widow's oil brought money with leftovers too.
(This method of multiplying we see Jesus teach,
While feeding five thousand with a boy's lunch on the beach.)

The Shunammite's Son

There was a couple whose name we know not;
They made for Elisha his very own spot.
So that he'd have a place when he would pass through,
They built him a room and furnished it too.
For them Elisha wanted to do something nice,
So he asked his servant to give him advice.
Elisha discovered the woman was reviled
Because she was barren and did not have a child.
So Elisha told her that she would have a son,
And by the next year this fulfillment was done.
Then one terrible day the little boy cried;
He'd hurt his head, and by noon he had died.
And just like Elijah on the dead boy he lay;
God brought him to life when he started to pray.

The Cure of Naaman

There was General Naaman from the Syrian state;
As commander-in-chief, his position was great.
He had leprosy and his future looked dim,
But his Hebrew slave girl gave some hope to him.
She said that Elisha could make leprosy well,
And so Naaman then traveled to Israel.
Elisha wouldn't see him or even come to the door;
This made Naaman angry, more than ever before.
Elisha sent out a message that made Naaman quiver;

He was to dip seven times in the Jordan River.
This was too foolish, and he wouldn't obey,
But his servant girl coaxed him to comply anyway.
After seven dips in the river, Naaman was healed,
And so was his pride, which Elisha revealed.

Gehazi's Greed

Now Naaman's heart was pricked to the core,
And he vowed that only God he'd adore.
He returned to Elisha to offer gifts from his wealth
In gratitude for his returning to health.
Elisha's servant, Gehazi, served only in deed,
For his heart was really ruled by greed.
Elisha refused Naaman's gifts for his healing;
This caused Gehazi's thoughts to start reeling.
Right after Naaman headed back to his land,
Gehazi ran after him with a tale so grand:
"My master Elisha is now asking of you
Gifts for two prophets soon to pass through.
He asked for silver and two changes of clothes,"
Thinking he's safe since nobody knows.
Naaman was more than glad to comply,
Not knowing Gehazi had told a big lie.
Gehazi returned and sneaked quietly inside
And looked for a place for his treasures to hide.
Elisha soon asked him, "Where have you been?
Do you think I don't know when you practice sin?
The sickness of Naaman unto you now shall cleave."
Gehazi turned white as snow and forever did leave.

The Syrians Tricked

The Syrians simply could not conquer small Israel
Because when they tried, Elisha could tell.
God told Elisha their secrets, and he told the King.
For the Syrian Army that botched everything.

So the Syrians plotted with their human mind;
They went to conquer Elisha, but God made them blind.
Elisha told them that they had gone astray,
But he'd gladly help them to find the right way.
So he led them right through his city gate;
This could have been such a terrible fate.
Elisha then asked God to open their eyes;
The Syrians weren't expecting this frightful surprise.
The king of Israel asked, "May we kill them all dead?"
Elisha said, "No, just see that they're fed."
Elisha said they should all be set free;
Israel saw no more of the Syrian Army.

Jonah

God spoke to Prophet Jonah one day:
"Announce that judgment is on the way
To the people of Nineveh who cause endless grief
Because their wickedness is beyond belief."
Jonah knew of the Ninevites' atrocities;
Why should God warn such people as these?
Knowing God's mercy, Jonah didn't obey
And jumped on a ship going the opposite way.
While on the journey the waves stormed and roared;
This was because of Jonah aboard.
Soon it was known to all of the crew
That to throw Jonah over was what they must do.
So the sailors threw Jonah into the sea,
And then God calmed the sea immediately.
God has His ways to accomplish His wish,
And Jonah was swallowed by a great fish.
For three days and three nights in the belly he stayed,
And during this time he repented and prayed.
On the third day the fish's belly was sore,
And the fish spewed out Jonah on the edge of the shore.

Jonah traveled quite far to get to Nineveh town;
Then he gave them God's message, not watered down.
He told the people that in forty more days
They'd be destroyed because of their evil ways.
The people repented and fell on their knees,
And the Lord God forgave them as He heard their pleas.
When the destruction of Nineveh didn't take place,
Jonah felt betrayed and suffered disgrace.
Then Jonah found shade under a gourd;
A worm cut it down, and Jonah was floored.
God said, "You cry about the shade for your head;
I'd rather you cry for My people instead."

Isaiah

Seven hundred years before Christ, a prophet we see
Who is one of the greatest in all history.
This young man, Isaiah, in Judah did dwell.
The way God called him is a story to tell:
One day in the temple, while all alone,
Isaiah saw a vision of God high on His throne.
He saw angel-like beings, called seraphim,
Worshiping God and shouting praises to Him.
Frightened Isaiah fell down in distress
And cried, "Woe is me, for I'm such a mess!
I say evil things, and my people speak lies."
All of his sins he began to despise.
From God's altar a seraph picked up a coal;
He touched Isaiah's lips, making him clean and whole.
God said, "Whom shall I send, who can he be?"
Isaiah answered, "Here I am, Lord, send me."
God gave him a message that was not well received;
When he delivered God's message, no one believed.
For many years Isaiah sang the same song,
"Turn back to God and repent of your wrong,
Or your enemies will conquer and take you away."
The people would not hear what he had to say.

Christ Prophesied

"Messiah" means: The One who's anointed
To fulfill the assignment God has appointed.
"Messiah" and "Christ" mean the same, so to speak;
"Messiah" is Hebrew, and "Christ" is the Greek.

Isaiah told of a messenger preparing the way;
It was John the Baptist, as we know today,
A voice in the wilderness, declaring God's word,
Calling all to repent and turn to the Lord.
On the coming of Christ, Isaiah had much to tell
Of One "Born of a virgin, called Immanuel,
Despised and rejected, scorned like a thief,
A man of sorrows and acquainted with grief.
Like a lamb He stood silent before His accusers
As He offered His life to save His abusers.
For all of our sins, He paid the fee;
He was wounded so we can be free.
For unto us a Child is born and a Son given,
And man's salvation comes down from Heaven,
To rule a kingdom that never will cease,
Wonderful Counselor, Mighty God, Prince of Peace.
A Descendant of David will sit on his throne
And rule with love His very own."

God made a promise that once seemed remote,
Which Prophet Isaiah was faithful to quote:
"Oh had you listened to My commands,
But I will rescue you from distant lands.
Those who hate you will suffer much shame.
They have cast you out because of My name.
But in one single day, in spite of the scorn,
Through the travail of Zion, a nation is born.
Delight in Jerusalem with a mother's desire."
But the wicked shall face God's fury and fire.

(Of this prophecy we now know the date;
Israel was born May, nineteen forty eight.)

Also Micah, who lived in the time of Isaiah,
Had this to say of the coming Messiah:
"You O, Bethlehem, shall see the birth
Of one who'll be honored to the ends of the earth.
He will bring peace to every land
And feed His flock by the strength of His hand."

The Fall of Lucifer

In *Isaiah* fourteen the prophet, God's friend,
Gives the history of Satan from beginning to end.
It is also written in *Ezekiel* twenty eight.
This is a summary of what they relate:
Lucifer was an archangel so bright;
In fact his name meant radiant light,
Shining star, son of the morning.
Jewels and music made up his adorning.
He led the hosts of Heaven in worship and praise,
But he became discontent in all of his ways,
Saying, "I'll take Heaven's throne away from the Lord;
It is I who should be praised and adored.
I will sit on the mount of God's congregation,
On the sides of the north, God's own habitation."
One third of the angels joined in rebellion;
Lucifer became the original hellion.
They were cast out of Heaven at God's command;
Then they set their sights on Earth's lovely land.
Satan became the archangel's new name;
This lovely world was never the same.
His agenda was to destroy and kill
And to get God's creation to bend to his will.
He would not stop until he set up his throne,
So that he could lord over all of God's own.
"One day," said Isaiah, "the whole world will stare,

'Can this be the one who brought such grief everywhere?
Is this the one who made people slaves,
Who destroyed the good and sent men to their graves?'
The very one who said, 'On God's throne I will sit'
Has now ended up in the bottomless pit.
Because of your beauty, you puffed up with pride.
You corrupted God's wisdom on every side."

CAPTIVITY

Israel 722 B.C.

Because no one listened to what the prophets did say,
Troubled times for Israel did not go away.
They worshiped their idols, so God let them fall,
And the Assyrians completely conquered them all.
The Israelites were taken to Assyria to dwell,
And since have been called the lost tribes of Israel.

Judah

God Destroys the Assyrian Army

The Assyrian army against Judah marched forth,
For now they had Israel and all lands south and north.
But with only two tribes, Judah was small,
So to conquer them should be no trouble at all.
King Sennacharib was their king of great might,
And on Jerusalem he'd set his sight.

Hezekiah was Judah's king of renown.
He ordered that all pagan shrines be torn down.
He collected gifts, what folks could afford,
So the priests could devote themselves to the Lord.

King Sennacharib threatened, "You'll be next."
He sent Judah a message, and this is the text:
"Hezekiah tells you that your God is strong

But I want to tell you that he is wrong!
King Hezekiah only leads you astray;
Nobody's god has stood in our way."
This message started to make people cower,
But Jerusalem's God is the true God of power.
Hezekiah spoke to his people: "Don't be afraid!
Our God is not by human hands made."

As Assyria was threatening to take Judah away,
Hezekiah asked old Isaiah to get busy and pray.
As Isaiah prayed, the message came through;
God said, "I will fight this battle for you."
The Angel of the Lord came that very night
And killed the Assyrians at their campsite.
It wasn't God's timing for Judah to fall.
As Hezekiah cried out, God answered his call.
Also the Assyrians were getting too proud;
They conquered Israel only because God had allowed.

Hezekiah Healed

During this time Hezekiah became very sick.
Isaiah told him to fix his affairs really quick,
For God had spoken that he was to die.
This news caused Hezekiah to grieve and to cry.
Hezekiah prayed, but it was Isaiah who heard;
He was to tell the king God's very word:
"I've heard your prayer and I've seen your tears,
I'll add to your life fifteen more years."
But Hezekiah said, "How shall I know;
How can I be sure if that's really so?"
So as proof he'd be healed of the disease,
Isaiah said God would move the sun ten degrees.
Hezekiah could choose which way it would move;
He chose it to go back if it were to prove.
So the sun went backward an exact ten degrees;
Only God can give us signs such as these.

Hezekiah had such a glorious start,
But later in life, pride seeped into his heart.
When an envoy from Babylon paid him a call,
He showed them his treasures, everything, all!
When Isaiah asked, "What have you done?
You've exposed yourself to the evil one.
Your land will be conquered and each son a slave.
This will not happen till you go to your grave."
Hezekiah rejoiced at what Isaiah said
Because these things wouldn't happen until he was dead.

Jeremiah and Ezekiel

Jeremiah's Call

In Judah was born an unusual child;
His manner was shy, and his temper was mild.
But when a young man of twenty years old,
God called Jeremiah to be a prophet so bold.
When Jeremiah said, "I'm too young and can't speak."
God touched his mouth, and he was no longer weak.
Jeremiah became strong; he'd rave and he'd shout
Until from the temple he was forever cast out.
He begged the people to repent of their sin,
For they were decaying right from within.
God said, "You worship idols before My very eyes.
You offer your children as a sacrifice.
You are filled with lust and refuse to repent.
Because of this, I cannot relent.
Babylon will attack and cause Judah's fall.
They'll besiege Jerusalem and break down the wall.
But if you surrender, things will go well."
For these words Jeremiah was locked in a cell.
The prophecy happened as Jeremiah had said;
Many were captured and many were dead.
The treasures were saved before the temple was burned
And carried to Babylon, to be one day returned.
Jerusalem was burned and left in a heap.

But God made a promise, one He would keep:
"Into foreign lands, you will scatter and roam
Until that time I call you back home.
Once again with people your land will be filled.
You will prosper and flourish as your soil is tilled.
Onto David's throne My Branch shall ascend.
With wisdom and truth He shall attend
To all of My flock who fill up the land;
His name is the Lord, My Righteous Right Hand."
Jeremiah was faithful in speaking God's word.
They had ears to hear, but nobody heard.

Ezekiel's Prophecy

Out of the North came four living creatures
With four sides to their heads and unlikely features--
A face of a man, an ox, lion and eagle.
They were the color of flames and amber so regal.
They grabbed Ezekiel, who was a priest by his birth,
And took him to a place between Heaven and Earth.
Then God spoke to Ezekiel of things yet to be:
(Things that have since happened in history)
"I will scatter My people in every direction,
And only in Me can they find true protection.
Then I'll gather them from the lands where they dwell;
And bring them back to their land, Israel.
I will give them one heart and a new spirit within;
They'll love My laws and no longer sin.
In foreign lands they will no longer trod;
They'll be My people, and I'll be their God."
The Glory departed as the creatures lifted their wings.
Ezekiel was hated for revealing these things.
Ezekiel saw the future for which God's people would yearn,
When the Glory of God would one day return.

The Valley of Dry Bones

Again, God's Spirit swept Ezekiel away
To a large valley where a stash of bones lay.
The Lord asked the prophet, "Can these bones revive?"
God told him to speak and they'd come alive.
So Ezekiel spoke, "You will live once again.
You will stand on your feet as an army of men."
A loud rattle ensued as the bones reconnected,
And with muscles and skin they were resurrected.
The four winds blew and filled them with breath;
No longer were they victims of death.
God said, "This is Israel who will once again stand,
And they will return to their own land. ✡
After they've seen what I plan to do,
Then they will know that My Promise is true."

Judah's Captivity/Jeremiah's Letter

Then in the year five-eighty-six B.C.
Babylonia took Judah into captivity.
Jeremiah was permitted in Judah to stay;
For being God's faithful servant, that was his pay.
The captives in Babylon wept many tears.
Jeremiah told them they'd be there seventy years.
He gave them advice in a wonderful letter,
Hoping that this would help them act better.
He said, "Build sturdy homes and plant lots of food,
And God will increase you and add to your brood.
God says, 'For this country I want you to pray,
So all of their blessings can come also your way.
I am the Lord over all of the world;
To you I have given My Holy Word.
When you cry out and turn back to Me,
I'll bring you back home and set you free.'"

Daniel

Nebuchadnezzar was Babylon's king then.
He was interested in the Jewish young men.
He wanted the healthy, polite and well-brained
To be brought to the palace so they could be trained.
He chose the best-looking, the cream of the crop,
So they could be officials and serve at the top.
He wanted them to forget whence they came,
So to each young man he gave a new name.

Daniel's Diet

One young man, Daniel, who did not want to be rude,
Did not want to eat the palace's food.
By Hebrew law these foods were "unclean",
But the servant in charge feared he'd get too lean.
Daniel and his three friends made a request:
Eating vegetables for ten days would be the test.
If after ten days they were healthy and strong,
They could eat "clean" food all the year long.
The simple test seemed to settle the matter,
For the four boys got stronger, taller, and fatter.

Nebuchadnezzar's Dream

In their studies the Lord gave them a hand,
And they became wiser than the best in the land.
The king had a dream that concerned him a lot,
So he called his wizards and put them on the spot:
"You must tell me the dream that I had in the night;
Only then will I know your interpretation is right."
They couldn't interpret a dream they didn't know,
So the king said, "Kill them all, and don't be slow!"
But when Daniel found out about the big task,
He said, "That is simple, for God I shall ask."
So he saved all the wizards from an awful fate.
As he told the king's dream, he began to relate:

"You dreamed of a statue of a man dazzling bright;
He was tall and strong, a man of great might.
His head was gold with silver arms and chest.
His belly was bronze and then the rest
Were legs of iron and feet mixed with clay.
A stone broke from a mountain and crashed it away.
Then the stone grew huge and covered the Earth.
The statue represents the four kingdoms of worth.
The nations were crumbled by God, who was the stone.
It meant God would set up a kingdom all of His own."

(As we look back in our world's history,
The nations described, we now clearly see.
Babylonia was portrayed as the head of gold;
The arms were the Medes and Persians of old.
The belly of bronze was the Greek civilization;
The iron and clay were the late Roman nation.
The small stone represented Christ at His birth.
The huge stone means that He'll rule the whole Earth.)

The Fiery Furnace

One day Nebuchadnezzar made a stupid plan:
He would build an image to be worshiped by man.
His workers made a gold statue ninety feet high;
Whoever refused to worship would die.
Into a furnace he would be cast
To be burned up completely in a fiery blast.
Daniel's three friends, whom we mentioned before,
Would not worship the idol; only God they'd adore.
Shadrach, Meshach and Abednego were the names of the three,
And they flatly refused to bow down their knee:
"Our God will save us, but that is not why,
Even if He doesn't, we'd rather die."
They were thrown into the furnace with a heat so intense
The soldiers burned up, for the flames were immense.
The king looked at the furnace and saw another One,

"Who," he said, "appears to be as God's Son."
He called them out of the fire, and with amazement he cried,
For the three were not touched, and they should have been fried.

The King's Dream about the Tree
King Nebuchadnezzar had another dream;
This one was different and had a new theme.
He dreamed of a tree in a large field;
The tree was huge and had a large yield.
Then a watching-angel came down from the sky
And cut down the tree that had been so high.
He scattered the leaves, and the birds flew away;
For seven years the stump would have to stay.
The stump would have a beast's heart and be covered with dew
Until it discovered that the Lord God is true.

Nebuchadnezzar asked Daniel what the dream meant;
Daniel begged the king to yield and repent.
Daniel said the tree was the king with treasures untold,
But soon he'd be living out in the cold.
Because he was so great in his own eyes,
The Lord would make him a king that all would despise.
He would become like a beast, and he would eat grass;
He'd be covered with dew, but all this would pass.
He would be restored because he'd know then
That the Lord gives us all and is the ruler of men.

One year later, while strolling his roof,
The king was still boasting and acting aloof.
Just as in the dream the Lord God had given,
King Nebuchadnezzar was from society driven.
The dream came true as Daniel said it would,
And the whole lesson did the king lots of good.
After seven years his mind was restored,
And he returned to his throne praising the Lord.

The Handwriting on the Wall

King Nebuchadnezzar passed on to glory;
Now his son, Belshazzar, enters the story.
Belshazzar was wicked and really a clod;
He threw a huge party and made fun of God.
He used the Temple goblets that had been stored
To toast the idols and blaspheme the Lord.
During the noise a hush suddenly did fall,
For a hand mysteriously appeared on the wall.
Everyone there was filled with great fright
As the hand on the wall started to write.
The king called the wizards to read what it said,
But they did not know, so they called Daniel instead.
Daniel then read, "Because of your deeds,
Your kingdom will fall to the Persians and Medes."
The king knew at once this message was right;
The king and his empire fell that very night.

The Lions' Den

King Cyrus of Persia then took the lead,
Soon to be followed by King Darius the Mede.
King Darius appointed Daniel to be in command
Over one hundred twenty princes who ruled the land.
These princes were a mean, jealous crew,
And to get rid of Daniel they pledged to do.
They secretly met, and a law they did pen
That was sure to put Daniel into the lions' den.
They knew Daniel prayed daily, for this they saw,
So it was about this that they made up a law.
It said, "If anyone prays to any god but the king,
It would be sure his destruction to bring."
The king signed the law for he didn't know
That it was a plot to kill Daniel, the one he loved so.
Daniel heard of the law, but he didn't obey;
He still prayed at his window three times every day.
The officials were watching, and Daniel got caught;

Then Daniel was to King Darius brought.
Darius was miserable because now he saw
That he had been tricked to sign such a law.
Darius wanted to save him, but his hands were tied;
"Your God will save you!" to Daniel he cried.
They fed Daniel to the lions, whose mouths were shut tight;
They could not touch him or take even one bite.

Darius was so upset that he could not sleep.
Would he find Daniel's bones all in a heap?
Darius went to the den and saw Daniel protected,
So he wrote a new law that Daniel's God be respected.
Darius was angry with those vicious men;
His accusers were thrown into the lions' den.
They were devoured in a minute or two,
And that was the end of that jealous crew.

Dream of the Four Beasts

One night while Daniel was lying in bed,
He had dreams and visions come into his head.
He saw four beasts come out of the sea;
They were as different as they could be:
The first like a lion and then one like a bear,
The third like a leopard with feathers for hair.
The fourth beast was dreadful, exceedingly terrible;
It had iron teeth, and its claws were unbearable.
The four different beasts were kingdoms so grand;
The last beast of all devoured the land.
It conquered the people with its iron jaws
And trampled God's saints with his terrible claws.
This last beast had ten horns on his head;
These were the kings that the beast led.
Then three horns were replaced by one mighty horn;
It was against this horn God wanted to warn.
He was boastful and proud, God's archenemy;
Only God Himself can set people free.

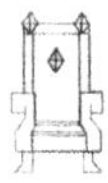

Then One came with thrones, called Ancient of Days,
His robe white as snow and His throne all ablaze.
He sat down to judge, and *The Books* were employed.
The fourth beast was killed and his body destroyed.
A Man came in the clouds; then the Ancient of Days
Gave Him dominion, and the Earth filled with praise.
Then one standing close to the throne's side,
Said, "Holy Days and God's law will be defied.
God's holy people will be vexed in their soul
As they are subjected to Evil's control.
But after three and a half years of pain,
God's holy people will rule and reign."

The Goat and Ram Vision

Daniel had several visions about days ahead;
There was a vision that filled him with dread.
He saw a goat and a ram in a vision one day
But did not understand what it was trying to say.
So the Angel Gabriel then did appear;
It was his mission to make this vision clear.
Again it was about the four kingdoms of power.
He spoke of the last ruler in the last hour:
"He shall cause much fear and use every ploy,
And all of God's people he shall try to destroy.
Deceit shall prosper under his hand;
He'll exalt himself and make himself grand.
No human on earth can destroy his power."
After Gabriel explained, Daniel's stomach felt sour.
God said, "The time is far off; don't reveal this yet."
Daniel wrote it all down, so he would not forget.

Seventy Weeks of Years

While Daniel was praying for his people, the Jews,
Again Gabriel came with prophetic news:
"In seventy weeks of years God's Holy One will come.
The first sixty-nine weeks make up the first sum.

In sixty-nine weeks of years, four-hundred-eighty-three,
The Anointed One will die for our iniquity. ✝
Jerusalem must be restored after the current fall;
The counting-time will start with the decree to build the wall.
For our sins the Messiah's life will quickly be cut short;
The destruction of the temple will confirm the whole report."
(We know that our Messiah came before year seventy A.D.,
For that is when the Temple fell as foretold in prophecy.)

"Many years would pass before the final week would come."
For one week of years, seven is the sum.
This will be the time John describes in Revelation,
When a feared one comes and destroys every nation.
"All transgression will be finished, and there'll be no more sin,
And everlasting righteousness at that time will begin."

RETURN FROM CAPTIVITY

The seventy years passed, and as Jeremiah had vowed,
That to rebuild the temple, they would be allowed.
For Cyrus was the king now, and righteous was he,
And because he loved God, he made a decree:
"God wants Jerusalem's temple rebuilt,
For God has forgiven the Jews' sin and guilt.
Anyone who wishes may return to their land,
And all who remain here can give them a hand
By giving their money, their goods and supplies."
So fifty thousand packed up and said their good-byes.
Cyrus returned the treasures Nebuchadnezzar had taken;
They belonged in the temple, which God had not forsaken.
Thousands stayed in Babylon, where their pleasures were many,
And did not go to Jerusalem, where there wouldn't be any.

Rebuilding the Temple and Wall

Zerubbable and Jeshua were to lead the great task;
Zerubbable was an ancestor of Jesus, should anyone ask.
They started to rebuild the temple with zeal,

But as time went on, the work lost its appeal.
The wall and temple were a discouraging sight;
Then the jealous Samaritans acted in spite.
When Artaxerxes became the next Persian king,
The Samaritans incited him to stop everything.
They sent the king a treacherous letter:
"With Jerusalem restored, things would never get better.
If the Jews build their city, they will surely rebel."
King Artaxerxes reaction was easy to tell.
He told the Samaritans their message was right,
So he stopped the Jews from rebuilding the site.

Haggai and Zechariah

Then two prophets, Haggai and Zechariah, spoke to the Jews.
Haggai said, "Your actions God finds hard to excuse.
You build yourselves homes while God's house is a mess,
And because of this, He will not bless."
Zechariah, too, encouraged the down-hearted,
Confirming Zerubbable would finish what he had started.
Then King Darius renewed Cyrus's decree.
This gave the Jews a new energy.
With his royal support the battle was won,
And rebuilding the temple finally was done.

Zechariah's Prophecy

Zechariah foretold of the king of each nation:
"Lowly, riding an ass and bringing salvation.
One day all nations against Jerusalem shall fight,
And this very King shall make everything right.
On the Mount of Olives this King shall stand,
And the Lord shall be King over every land."
(We've seen this King lowly and riding an ass
As the people waved palms while letting him pass.
And we'll see him again at the unknown hour
When he returns releasing his mighty power.)

Nehemiah

Twelve years later we see Artaxerxes' top man,
Nehemiah, a noble from Judah's clan.
He was close to the king and one day looked sad;
This was unusual for he always looked glad.
The king asked Nehemiah, "Why are you sad?"
Nehemiah said, "It's because of Jerusalem; the news is so bad.
The neighbors are plundering, and the gates have been burned;
The walls are in ruins and are all over-turned.
It is my prayer to go there and rebuild."
The king then declared his prayer was fulfilled.
He gave Nehemiah his royal protection,
And from the king's forest, he could have his selection.
Nehemiah journeyed far to get to the site;
He inspected the walls on the third night.

They started working, and the conditions were hard;
One half would build, and one half would guard.
The Samaritans relentlessly used every scheme,
But they could not outwit Nehemiah's fine team.
They tried to kill the workers and break down the wall;
They tried to trick Nehemiah, but he didn't fall.
In fifty-two days the wall was complete,
And the Samaritans left; they knew they were beat.

Ezra

While in Jerusalem the Jews ran with the wrong crowd;
They married pagan women, which was not allowed.
A priest named Ezra, who in Babylon stayed,
Was so upset he cried out and prayed.
He asked permission from Artaxerxes, the king,
Who told Ezra to go and let God's message ring:
"Teach them God's law and His righteous path,
For why should we risk incurring God's wrath?"

With the temple rebuilt and the walls now restored,
It was time to renew the word of the Lord.

They carefully prepared for that special day,
When all would assemble to hear what God had to say.
When Ezra arrived, he preached loud and strong:
"We must turn back to God and repent of our wrong.
Our worship of idols is an abomination
And has been the cause of our relocation.
Our pagan wives have led us astray;
We must divorce them and send them away.
Now we are slaves in our ancestors' land
And are governed by a foreigner's hand.
As our days of captivity come to an end,
We have sinful ways we must face and amend."
Ezra read from the scrolls, and the people learned much;
With the laws and the holy days they were so out of touch.
They worshiped and wept with a heart to obey
And said, "It's our duty to do as you say."
Nehemiah spoke, saying, "You must not grieve
But celebrate with joy because you believe."

Malachi

Malachi is the last prophet we see,
Foretelling events that are now history:
"The Lord whom you seek, in whom you delight,
Will suddenly come and make everything right.
Like a fire that refines and like fuller's soap,
He will bring justice to those without hope."
All through the Old Testament, God laid the foundation
For the birth of His Son who would bring man's salvation.

JOB, RUTH AND ESTHER

Three Old Testament books are important to mention;
Job, Ruth, and Esther deserve special attention.
As the oldest of books, Job's story is grand.
Ruth's story took place when judges ruled the land.
Esther became queen, ascending to royalty
During the time of Judah's captivity.

Job

Job was a good man with an invisible hedge,
So Satan asked God to give him an edge.
Satan said, "Job loves you because he's so blessed;
I ask permission to give him a test.
If Job's many blessings are taken away,
He will curse You from that very day."
God said, "Although Job's fortunes should quickly reverse,
Job is faithful, and he never would curse."
Both Satan and God had something to prove;
So Job's hedge of protection God did remove.

Satan destroyed Job's children and wealth;
Job's wife was spared, but Job lost his health.
Job cried out to God and continued to cleave,
Saying, "Naked I was born, and naked I'll leave."
Job suffered boils all over his skin.
His friends assumed it was caused by some sin.
Three of Job's friends begged him to confess,
"You must surely be sinful if your life's such a mess."
But Job said, "You don't understand my situation,
Only God can give illumination.
    I know that my redeemer lives;
    One day He'll stand upon this sod.
    Though this body will decay,
    Yet in my flesh I shall see God.
The Lord knows the way of those in His fold;
When He has tried me, I shall come forth as gold."
Job held out for God, his only source,
For the opinions of friends just threw him off course.
Finally one day the Lord God came through.
He said, "Job, I have some questions for you."
Job had no answers, and he could not speak;
When he saw God's wisdom, he became weak.
Job said, "With my ears I have heard about Thee,
But now, at last, with my eyes I can see."

God told Job's friends that they'd gone astray,
And He would forgive them if Job would pray.
So Job prayed for his friends, and they were restored.
Job was greatly honored by the hand of the Lord.
Job's sickness left; he now had his health.
Job had more children and doubled his wealth.
Our trusting God is what gives Him glory,
For only God knows the end of the story.

Ruth

A man named Elimelech, from Bethlehem town,
Moved his family to Moab when famine came down.
Then the man died, leaving two sons and a wife;
The sons married Moabites and got on with their life.
Both sons died, and the three women were left;
With no means of support, they were so bereft.
Naomi, the mother, moved back to Bethlehem's way;
One daughter-in-law left; one decided to stay.
That one was Ruth, who was faithful and true;
She said to Naomi, "I will never leave you."
Naomi said, "I have nothing to offer,
No means of support to fill up your coffer."
Ruth said, "Entreat me not to leave from your side;
Wherever you go, I shall abide.
Your very own people shall become mine;
I shall be a servant of your Lord God divine.
And when my life on this earth is through,
I shall be buried right beside you."

Because Ruth and Naomi had nothing to eat,
Ruth worked in a field gleaning barley and wheat.
Boaz, the owner, was a good, godly man;
He was a relative of Elimelech's clan.
When Boaz saw Ruth, he liked what he saw,
And he heard of her kindness to her mother-in-law.
Ruth impressed Boaz, and he spoke with affection,

"Please glean from my fields and receive my protection."
He told the reapers to drop some of their yield,
So Ruth could easily glean from his field.

Naomi told Ruth to apply oils so sweet
And go in at night and lay at Boaz's feet.
When Boaz awoke, he did so esteem her,
He vowed to become Ruth's kinsman redeemer.

Naomi had Elemilech's property for sale;
There were many customs that had to prevail.
Who bought the land would have Ruth for a wife
To have children in honor of Elimelech's life.
Boaz would be the second in line
To purchase the land if the first should decline.
Elimelech's brother declined, so Boaz purchased the land,
And in marriage he took Ruth's lovely hand.
Ruth bore him Obed, her very first son,
Whose offspring was Jesse, who fathered David to come.
Ruth's faithfulness is noted in all history;
Her name is recorded in Christ's family tree.

Esther

When the Persian Queen Vashti caused her husband disgrace,
Lovely Esther was chosen to take Vashti's place.
Mordacai, Esther's cousin, learned of a plot toward the king.
He promptly told Esther, who exposed the whole thing.
One day in the future the king would recall
And honor Mordacai for preventing his fall.

Queen Esther didn't know that behind the scene
The Prime Minister, Haman, was greedy and mean.
Since Mordacai, a Jew, refused to bow to that man,
Haman wanted to kill him and the whole Jewish clan.
So he tricked King Xerxes to sign a decree
That would destroy the Jews mercilessly.

When Mordacai heard this, he went to the queen
And sent a strong message that she must intervene:
"Perhaps you are queen to provide a solution,
For a time such as this, to stop our execution."
Even though Esther was the king's wife,
Addressing this issue could endanger her life.
So Esther asked the Jews to fast and to pray
Before approaching the king to ask for a say.
As she entered the throne room, the king gave permission,
So Esther proceeded to ask him a question,
"I would be honored to prepare dinner for you.
Would you please come and bring Haman too?"
The king gladly accepted her kind invitation.
Haman, too, was filled with elation.
After the banquet, Haman felt very exalted,
But when he passed Mordecai, he was once more insulted.
So Haman's wife and friends said, "Build a tall gallows,
Then tomorrow you can hang that Mordacai fellow."

That very night, before the king went to bed,
He asked for the *Book of Deeds* to be read.
It told how Mordacai gave information
Which saved the king from extermination.
The king then made a quick resolution
To honor Mordacai for this great contribution.
Just then, Haman appeared to discuss Mordacai
And to make arrangements for him to die.
Before Haman could speak, the king asked a question,
Asking him to give a suggestion,
"Please tell me, Haman, what I could plan
If I wanted to honor and thank a good man."
Haman replied with vigor and vim,
Assuming the king was referring to him,
"Clothe that man in the king's royal gown,
Let him ride the king's horse all through the town."
The king replied, "That's exactly what I shall do!

Mordacai is the man; I'll leave arrangements to you."
The very day Haman planned to put Mordacai down,
He was made to parade him all through the town.

Haman was already getting nervous and scared
When he was whisked to a next meal Esther prepared.
Esther laid a fine banquet, her very best.
The king was so pleased, he said, "Make any request."
Esther was ready; that was all she needed.
Then for her life she tearfully pleaded.
She exposed Haman's plan to kill every Jew.
The king was enraged, and Haman was through.
On the gallows he built to hang Mordacai,
Haman was promptly sentenced to die.
The king learned that Mordacai was Esther's relation,
And he made him Prime Minister over the nation.

Since a king's decree can't be changed ever,
The king had a solution that was very clever.
The Jews were allowed, before the attack,
To prepare for the battle so they could fight back.
When the great day of battle finally arrived,
The heathen were slaughtered, but the Jews all survived.
The Jews now remember these days with great cheer,
And two days of Purim are honored each year.

THE NEW TESTAMENT

THE LIFE OF JESUS THE CHRIST

Four hundred years passed between the Old Testament and New,
And in a short span of time many prophecies came true.
God's timing was perfect, and the way had been made;
Rome ruled the world; new roads had been laid.
Communication was easy for most people could speak
A common language that was established in Greek.
And now at this time God was ready to move;
His great love for us, He was ready to prove.

The Gospels of Matthew, Mark, Luke, and John
Teach us of Jesus, God's Promised One.
Matthew, Mark, and Luke give us a look
As Christ's life is revealed in God's Holy Book.
John gives a spiritual view that's so fresh,
How the Word was God and the Word became flesh.

The Birth of Jesus

Zachariah and Elizabeth, an elderly pair,
Had suffered much sorrow for she could not bear.
They had prayed many years, for they wanted a son,
But because they were old, this could never be done.
Once a year the Jews for their sins would atone,
And Zachariah was chosen to go in all alone
To the Holy of Holies where he would repent,

And at the altar, he would burn a sweet scent.
While at the altar an angel did appear;
Zachariah was troubled and filled with fear.
It was Gabriel, the angel, and his message was clear;
Their prayers were answered for the Lord God did hear:
"Your wife Elizabeth will bear you a son.
He'll be a great man of God, and you must call him John.
He shall not drink strong drink, nor drink any wine;
He shall be filled with God's Holy Spirit divine.
For the coming of the Lord, He'll prepare the way
And turn hearts to the Lord for that special day."
Zachariah found this message hard to receive,
And he became dumb because he did not believe.

Six months after Elizabeth conceived her son,
The angel Gabriel appeared to another one--
A virgin named Mary, betrothed to be wed,
As Gabriel approached her, here's what he said:
"Hail Mary, you are God's favored one;
You will conceive in your womb and bear a son.
To the throne of King David, He shall ascend
To rule a kingdom that never will end.
He will be the Son of the Lord God Most High."
"How is that possible?" was Mary's reply.
"The Holy Spirit will come upon you."
And Mary believed and said, "Let it be true."
"Soon your cousin, Elizabeth, will deliver a son,
For when God speaks, you can consider it done.
She will confirm that my words are true.
There is nothing that the Lord cannot do."

With haste Mary went to Elizabeth's place
Where she wouldn't be judged or suffer disgrace.
Zachariah and Elizabeth knew the prophecies well,
Of the coming Messiah called Emanuel.
This was a storm they could gladly weather

Because they were all in this together.
Elizabeth, now being six months along,
When she saw Mary, burst forth as in song:
"Blessed are you and the fruit of your womb;
My babe leapt inside as you entered the room.
Blessed are you because you believed,
And all that was spoken shall be received."
Then Mary burst forth and began to relate:
"The Lord has regarded my lowly estate.
Now all generations shall call me blessed,
For I have been chosen among all the rest.
My soul rejoices in my Savior and Lord,
For He lifts up the humble and scatters the proud.
As He spoke to Abraham and his blessed seed,
The Lord gives to Israel the mercy they need."
After three months Mary's visit was done.
Elizabeth gave birth to her baby son.
Zachariah wrote down, "His name is John,"
And instantly his dumbness was totally gone.
Then Zachariah poured forth with a word:
"Blessed is he who prepares the way of the Lord.
His knowledge will lead people to peace,
And for those in darkness, light will increase."

When Joseph learned that his betrothed was with child,
He was deeply hurt, bewildered and riled.
So he decided to end his betrothal plight,
But Gabriel came in a dream to Joseph one night.
Gabriel told Joseph not to be afraid,
And that Mary was chosen as God's special maid:
"The child within Mary is God's only Son;
Now you must listen to what must be done.
The boy must be named Jesus," the angel said.
So Joseph took Mary, and then they were wed.
However in Bethlehem they had to be
For a census to be taken by Caesar's decree.

So to Bethlehem they journeyed with care,
For it was now time for Mary to bear.
After their journey they could find no place to stay,
So they stayed in a stable with the lambs and the hay.
(God didn't want His Son to be born in an inn,
For he was the Lamb who would die for our sin.)

In the stillness of night the Lord entered this world;
No trumpets were blown, no flags were unfurled.
There was no fanfare for our Creator and King;
He came as a babe, just a wee little thing.
He came to this Earth for a season to dwell;
He quietly entered, Emanuel.

As shepherds were watching their flocks in the night,
An angel appeared, and they were all filled with fright.
The angel said, "There is no need to fear;
I bring you good tidings, news of great cheer.
For Christ the Savior is born on this day
In the City of David, in a manger he lay."
Then a host of angels filled up the sky,
Singing glory to God in the heaven so high.
Their voices rang out in the night cold and still;
They sang of peace on Earth to men of good will.
The shepherds picked up their staffs and ran to the site,
And they told of the angels appearing that night.
Mary stored these things deep in her heart,
For in her life they would play a great part.

In the East some wise men saw a great star,
And they journeyed long, for the distance was far.
They knew that the star was a great sign
For the birth of a king, for someone divine.
When they reached Jerusalem, they spread the news
By asking, "Where is the one born King of the Jews?"
Herod then learned about this baby-boy rival

And started to worry about his own survival.
The priests said that Bethlehem was the best place to look,
For it had been prophesied in God's Holy Book.
Herod said, "When you find the child, report back to me,
So I, too, can show honor and bow down my knee."
The star led the wise men to Bethlehem;
Then the star stopped moving right over them.
They found the child and Mary, as they had been told,
And gave the babe gifts of myrrh, incense and gold.
(How wise those wise men turned out to be:
To the King of all kings, they bowed down their knee.)
In a dream God told them, "Ignore Herod's command,
And take a new route as you go back to your land."

Jesus' Childhood

From the time of His birth, Jesus was hidden away.
Even Satan was confused by what the prophets did say.
Fearing Jesus' birth was prophecy fulfilled,
King Herod ordered to have all baby boys killed.
But Joseph was warned in a dream to take flight,
So they fled to Egypt in the darkness of night.
There they remained until Herod's death,
And after, returned to the town Nazareth.

When Jesus was twelve the family went down
To celebrate the Passover in Jerusalem town.
When the days were fulfilled, their caravan left
To journey back home to Nazareth.
At the end of the day Jesus could not be found,
So Joseph and Mary turned right around.
After three days they found their Son in the temple,
Answering questions both complex and simple.
Although the scholars were duly impressed,
Joseph and Mary were very distressed.
Mary asked, "Son, why did you deal such a blow?"
Jesus said, "I must tend to God's work; I thought you'd know."

And again Mary stored these things in her heart.
At last reunited, they could finally depart.
Jesus grew strong in body and mind,
And in favor with God and also mankind.

Spiritual Law

About the life of Jesus, what can one say?
For redemption could have happened no other way.
Jesus had to fulfill every part of the law
To take back the captives without one single flaw.
To be born of a virgin was the heart of The Plan,
For by Spiritual Law sin is passed through the man.
And by Spiritual Law only blood can wash sin--
Water washes the outside; only blood washes within.
The blood of lambs and cattle can cover a lot,
But it cannot remove the tiniest spot.
It was the son of God, Adam, who brought on the curse,
And only a Son of God could make it reverse.
By the Lord's sinless life, the law was fulfilled,
And atonement accomplished when His blood was spilled.

It is our sin that makes Satan so bold,
But when sin is gone, Satan looses his hold.
For the wages of sin is no less than death;
It promises fun, but it robs every breath.
Sin is no joke; it makes your soul hide;
Even before death, you start dying inside.

Jesus' Ministry

Jesus Baptized

At thirty years old, by His Father's decision,
It was time for Jesus to proceed with His mission.
"Come and be baptized and repent of your sin,"
Shouted John the Baptist above society's din.
Jesus started His ministry by being baptized.
John the Baptist, His cousin, was really surprised:

"I baptize You? You should be baptizing me!"
Jesus answered him, "That is how it must be."
The Spirit descended, coming down like a dove,
And Jesus heard these words from His Father above:
"You are My Beloved Son; on You My favor rests";
Thus He was prepared for the following tests.

Satan Tempts Jesus

Jesus went into the wilderness to fast and to pray.
Forty days was the length of His stay.
Satan approached Him with conniving temptation,
And Jesus withstood him without hesitation.
"If You are God's Son, make bread from this stone."
Jesus said, "Man does not live by bread alone,
But by God's word, which is bread to the soul."
Satan continued with his evil goal;
He took Jesus to the temple roof high:
"If You jump from here, You will not die,
For You have angels assigned to protect.
You can jump safely without getting wrecked."
Jesus told Satan, that devilish clod,
"You shall not tempt the Lord your God."
Then Satan showed Jesus all the wealth of the land:
"All of these riches, I will put into Your hand.
If You worship me and bow at my feet,
I'll make Your life wealthy and sweet."
Jesus replied with vigor and verve:
"Worship God only, and only Him serve."
When Jesus spoke scripture, Satan was foiled;
Satan's hope to tempt Jesus was totally spoiled.
But Satan's not one to cut any slack;
At the next opportunity he would strike back.

After Satan relented and went on his way,
Jesus went to the synagogue on Sabbath Day.
He read from chapter sixty-one of *Isaiah*,

Which describes the ministry of the Messiah:
"God's Spirit is on Me to preach to the poor,
To bind broken hearts and open the prisoner's door."
After He read, Jesus was seated,
Saying to all, "Today these words are completed."
The people were thinking, "This Man is the One!"
Until someone said, "He's just Joseph's son."
Their admiration soon turned to hate,
So the people pushed Jesus out of the gate.
They tried to kill Him, but He slipped through the mob.
Then Jesus left Nazareth to get on with His job.

Friends and Disciples

Jesus gathered His disciples, twelve men in all;
As He walked by, they answered His call.
He would teach these men the Plan of Salvation;
One day they would take it to every nation.

Peter and Andrew were casting nets into the sea;
Jesus walked by and said, "Follow Me."
Then while walking a little further on,
He called two more brothers; they were James and John.
These four fishermen, who were unlearned and strong,
Put down their nets when the Lord came along.

Impetuous Peter was really Simon by name;
He'd speak so quickly, but his actions were lame.
Jesus asked His disciples, "What have you found?
What is the word that is going around?"
Jesus had clearly inspired much speculation,
For the disciples replied without hesitation,
"Some say You're Elijah, the prophet of old;
Some say John the Baptist or Jeremiah so bold."
Knowing He was the Promise of Abraham,
Jesus asked them, "Who do you say that I am?"
Peter spoke up with nary a prod,

"You are the Christ, the true Son of God."
"Blessed are you Simon for you're speaking true;
The Heavenly Father has revealed this to you."
Christ then named him Peter, meaning The Rock,
For this truth is the Church's first building block.
Then Jesus told them that He would have to die.
"Never Lord, never!" was Peter's hasty reply.
Jesus rebuked Satan and put him to flight,
For Peter's reaction was simply not right.
Peter the apostle was Jesus' great friend;
He promised he'd follow Him right to the end.
But when the soldiers took Jesus one night,
Peter denied Him, he was filled with such fright.
After the resurrection Jesus met him by the sea.
Three times Jesus asked Peter, "Do you love Me?"
Three times Peter denied Him, but now he could say,
"I love You my Master, and I want to obey."

John, the Beloved, was known to love Jesus the best.
At the last supper John laid his head on His breast.
Peter, James and John had a special relation;
They were present with Jesus at the transfiguration.
They climbed a mountain, and a great cloud so white
Surrounded them all, and Jesus' face became bright.
They saw Elijah and Moses speak to Jesus at length,
For His trial was near, and He would need extra strength.

Judas the apostle, who was greedy and weak,
Betrayed Jesus one night with a kiss on the cheek.

After the resurrection Thomas, who was quite a spouter,
Said, "Jesus can't be alive!" He's called 'Thomas the Doubter'.
When Jesus appeared, Thomas did finally perceive.
"Blessed are they," Jesus said, "who don't see, yet believe."

Mary, Martha, and Lazarus: two sisters, one brother,
Were a family to Jesus unlike any other.

When Jesus went to their home, Mary sat at His feet;
One day she anointed Him with oils so sweet.
Martha would cook meals and make lots of fuss.
With them Jesus could be "just one of us".
One day when busy Martha was preparing to eat,
Mary, wanting to listen, sat at Jesus' feet.
So Martha complained, "It just isn't fair
Because my sister isn't doing her share."
Then Jesus spoke clearly to Martha's stressed heart,
"Martha, my dear, Mary chose the best part."
About their friendship so much could be said;
When Lazarus died, Jesus raised him from the dead.

There was Mary Magdalene, who had seven devils cast out,
Who became a most faithful friend and followed Jesus about.

Jesus Turns Water to Wine

Jesus' first miracle turned out so fine,
The time when Jesus turned water to wine.
Jesus went to a wedding just to have fun;
Mary informed Him that the wine was all done.
She asked Jesus to help, but He was resistant,
But Mary, His mother, was very insistent.
Mary took all of the servants aside:
"Do all Jesus tells you," she whispered with pride.
So Jesus helped them with their concerns,
Saying, "Fill up with water all of your urns."
Then came the moment for the big test!
The host tasted the water, saying, "This wine is the best!"
(This miracle brought the celebration much peace,
And was also prophetic of the Spirit's release.)

Miracles and Teachings

Jesus taught Kingdom truths wherever He went.
Most people could see that He was Heaven sent:
He healed the crippled and made them to walk;
He healed the deaf, and then they could talk.

He healed the eyes of people born blind;
He delivered the demonized back to a sound mind.
By His power, broken people were mended,
And He stopped every funeral He ever attended.
Wherever Jesus went, people gathered around,
And wherever He taught, large crowds could be found.
Jesus healed men's bodies, and He healed their soul;
He showed that God wants us to be set free and whole.
He taught that your heart is the real you,
And that God sees your motives, not just what you do.
He wants to infuse us with His life and breath,
So that we will no longer be victims of death.
He wants us to live in the happy here-after,
No more troubles or sorrows but with joy and laughter.
When Jesus spoke, He made every word count,
As in the immortal Sermon on the Mount:

The Beatitudes and Lord's Prayer

"Blessed are the merciful, and blessed are the meek,
And those who thirst for God with a heart to seek.
Blessed are the righteous who always thirst for more;
God shall supply them from His ample store.
Blessed are those who mourn, for God shall them uphold.
Blessed are the pure in heart, for God they shall behold.
Blessed are the peacemakers as they walk upon this sod;
Each one of them shall be called a child of God.
Blessed are you when, for My sake, you're reviled;
This only proves that you truly are God's child.
You must forgive and bless your enemy;
Then you can walk in real victory.
You'll carry God's Kingdom wherever you go;
That is the best way for people to know."

The disciples asked Jesus to teach them to pray.
These are the words He taught them to say:
"Heavenly Father, praise Your holy name.
As it is in Heaven, let Earth be the same.

Give us this day the bread that we need;
Away from temptation we ask You to lead.
Deliver us from the works of the devil.
May we forgive all those who do evil
As we ourselves have been forgiven.
Glory and power are Yours in the Kingdom of Heaven."

More Truths

"Seek God's Kingdom first; be faithful and true,
And all that you need shall be added to you.
Fear not, little Flock, it's the Father's good pleasure
To give you the Kingdom, and that without measure.
When the world's treasures pass through your palms,
Your safest investment is to give it in alms.
The key to God's Kingdom is that you believe;
That is the secret for you to receive.
In this dark world, you are the light;
You are the salt to preserve what is right.
Speak God's word and give it a voice;
Speak to that mountain; don't give it a choice."

"When God gives you a talent, don't put it in store;
You must use it wisely; then He'll give you more.
If you bury your talent and don't make it increase,
You'll lose what you have, and your goods will decrease."

"If you have a problem with your sister or brother,
Tell them about it and not every other.
If he listens to you, then you've gained his heart,
But if he doesn't, you may let him depart."

"Don't judge another, and this is why:
You can't help a person with a log in your eye.
Don't take offense for offenses will come;
The world will think you are foolish and dumb.
When others abuse and do evil to you,

Don't let this tempt you to act that way too.
It's your inner thoughts that cause you to sin,
Thoughts of hatred and lust that come from within."

"Protect little children; help them walk a safe path;
Whoever harms them will suffer God's wrath."

Jesus said, "I was sick, and you visited Me,
When I was in prison, you helped set Me free.
When I was naked, you clothed My back.
You gave Me food when I suffered lack."
You may ask, "Lord, how can this be?"
"What you do for others, you do unto Me.
When you fail to show another respect,
I am the One that you really neglect."

Jesus Heals the Leper

As Jesus was traveling throughout Galilee,
A leper approached Him most courageously.
At Jesus' feet the poor leper fell,
"Lord, if you want to, you can make me well."
"I want to," said Jesus and then said, "Be healed.
Now show the priest, and let this truth be revealed."

Jesus Heals the Paralytic

Jesus went to Capernaum to visit a friend,
And it didn't take long for a crowd to descend.
When a paralyzed man, whose friends wouldn't forsake him,
Heard that Jesus was near, the friends wanted to take him.
When they got to the house, such a large crowd was reeling,
They dislodged the roof and lowered him through the ceiling.
When Jesus saw the man's faith, and how he was driven,
Jesus said, "Son take heart! Your sins are forgiven."
The religious who heard this were shocked and appalled,
Saying, "No one has the right to forgive sins except God."
Jesus asked when he saw some of them balk,

"Is it easier to say 'you're forgiven' or 'get up and walk'?
Since My power over sin, you refuse to believe,
I'll show you something that you can perceive."
Jesus then told the man, "Arise and pick up your mat."
The paralytic was healed just as quickly as that!
The healed man made his way through the crowd;
"We've never seen such a thing," they all said out loud.

A Most Extraordinary Day

A day in the life of the Lord was not dull.
The disciples learned this when they answered His call.
Jesus said, "Let us go to the other side of the lake,"
So they found for themselves a boat they could take.
They launched forth in the boat; Jesus fell fast asleep.
But after they had sailed out into the deep,
A violent wind quickly came down.
The disciples woke Jesus saying, "Master, we'll drown!"
Jesus arose and rebuked the wind and the sea,
And all became calm immediately.
Jesus scolded them for the fear they displayed;
His men marveled at how the wind and sea had obeyed.

When the disciples and Jesus reached the Gadarene shore,
A demonized man did loudly implore,
"O Son of God, are you here to torment?"
He lived in the tombs, and his cloths had been rent.
With demonic strength, he could break every chain,
And he'd cut his own body and cry out in pain.
This demonized man was feared in this region;
He had so many devils, they called themselves "Legion".
"Don't send us to the pit," the demons frantically cried,
"But into the pigs, feeding on the hillside."
Jesus agreed then told the demons to scram.
Two thousand pigs quickly became deviled ham.
Instantly from the hillside, the whole herd ran down
Into the lake where they were all drowned.

When the herdsmen saw what was just done,
They ran to the city to tell everyone.
So a crowd came to see. And what did they find?
They found the man fully clothed and in his right mind.
The crowd of people started to fear
And told Jesus to leave, to 'get out of here'.
Jesus told the healed man to return to his town
And tell what had happened to all people around.

When Jesus returned, an awaiting crowd was quite thick.
Jairus approached Jesus saying, "My daughter is sick."
He was a synagogue ruler and fell at the Lord's feet.
The people were thronging as they walked down the street.
Jesus cried out, "Who touched Me?" The disciples replied,
"Master, the people are pressing You on every side."
"No, somebody touched Me for I did perceive;
When someone is healed, I can feel power leave."
Trembling, a woman confessed, "Lord, it was I;
I touched only Your hem as You were passing by.
I was totally healed from twelve years of bleeding;
Only You could have given the help I was needing.
I have spent my money, all of my wealth,
But no doctors were able to restore me to health."
Jesus said, "Go in peace, your faith made you well."
Then a messenger arrived with sad news to tell:
"There's no need to bother the Master," he cried;
"It is too late, for your daughter has died."
Jesus said to Jairus, "Don't be afraid;
Just trust Me; I'll tend to your little maid."
At the house a crowd was wailing and weeping,
But Jesus told them the girl was just sleeping.
They laughed at Jesus, but he didn't bother;
He took James, Peter, and John; and the mother and father.
They went to the room where the daughter lay dead:
"Arise, My child," with a loud voice Jesus said.
Immediately the little girl got up from the bed.

Jesus instructed that she should be fed.
He told the stunned parents not to spread it about.
(But how could the people not have found out?)

Jesus Sends Out His Disciples

Jesus said to His twelve, "You've seen what I do;
I give you authority, now go out two by two.
Don't take money or bag, just your walking stick;
Cast out evil spirits, and heal the sick.
When you enter a village, stay in just one abode;
Let your hosts bless you as you travel this road.
If you are not welcomed at the village gate,
Shake the dust off your feet, and leave them to their fate.
I am sending you out as sheep among wolves;
Be as wise as serpents and harmless as doves."
So the disciples set out, urging all to repent,
And healing all the oppressed wherever they went.
After that, Jesus sent out another seventy two,
Saying, "The harvest is plenty but the workers are few.
I give you authority on serpents to trample;
You'll find My protection will always be ample."
When they came back, they were filled with such awe,
They continued to marvel at the things that they saw.
Jesus praised His Father with joy and delight
That God works through His children with power and might.

Parables about the Seed

Jesus taught many parables concerning the seed:
"It can yield good fruit but also the weed.
It can fall on hard rock or in deep, rich soil;
Birds can snatch it away or else it can spoil.
Worry and fret will act like a weed,
With one sure result: to strangle the seed.
A small, tiny seed can produce a big tree
With a home for the birds and a harvest for thee.
The smallest of seed has the power to grow--

Whether evil or good, you reap what you sow.
The Word of God is the incorruptible seed;
When planted in hearts, it supplies every need.
At the end of the age, when the weeds are mature,
And the wheat is ripe and strong to endure,
The angels will gather all the wheat and the weeds.
The weeds will be burned for their evil deeds.
The righteous wheat will shine like the sun,"
And Christ will proclaim, "The harvest is done."

Counting the Cost

When a man finds God's Kingdom, the pearl of great price,
He will not hesitate or even think twice.
He'll sell all he has so that he can afford
To attain the great pearl and follow the Lord.
Jesus never called the weak or faint hearted;
He calls those who'll finish what they have started:
"If you look back while you're plowing the sod,
You are not fit for the Kingdom of God.
If I call your name to come follow Me,
Don't ask permission from your family.
If you are ashamed to say that I am your friend,
Neither will I know you in the end.
If you stand up for Me, no matter the cost,
Nothing you've gained shall ever be lost.
Broad is the way and wide is the gate
To the path of destruction, where most congregate.
The Path of Life is narrow and straight,
And only a few choose to enter its gate."

John the Baptist Beheaded

When news about Jesus reached King Herod's ear,
The king was tormented with worry and fear.
His father, also King Herod, (whom we still scorn),
Had the baby boys killed when Jesus was born.
Herod Junior thought Jesus might be John resurrected,

So he asked his advisors and was soundly corrected.
John the Baptist had rebuked Herod's adulterous life,
So he imprisoned the Baptist at the request of his wife.
His wife really belonged to another;
She was married to Philip, King Herod's brother.
Herod's stepdaughter danced a beautiful dance
For King Herod's birthday, and the guests were entranced.
Herod said to the girl, "I will grant any wish."
She asked for John's head to be served on a dish.
When Herod saw that his vow was absurd,
It was too late to go back on his word.

John's disciples carried his body away.
When Jesus heard, He went alone just to pray.
Jesus and His disciples went off in a boat
To find a place that was alone and remote.
From many villages, people followed by land
And waited for Jesus till His boat reached the sand.
When Jesus saw their great needs and heard their pleas;
He stepped out of the boat and healed all their disease.

Feeding Five Thousand

The crowd followed Jesus wherever He went
Until they were tired, hungry and spent.
Jesus knew how to handle this poor, hungry bunch;
He fed the five thousand with a little boy's lunch.
How did He do that? From what witnesses say,
He blessed a boy's lunch and then gave it away.
From two fish and five loaves the people were fed,
With twelve baskets left of the fish and the bread.
The satisfied people went on their homeward way,
And Jesus stayed in the hills to be quiet and pray.
He had to take time to be quiet and still
To talk with the Father and know His perfect will.

Peter Walks on the Water

Jesus told His disciples not to abide
But to cross over the sea to the other side.
In the darkness of night a wind started to blow,
And the size of the waves started to grow.
When Jesus' disciples were miles from the coast,
They saw a man walking and thought it was a ghost.
With fearful shouts, they started to cry;
Then they heard Jesus say, "Fear not, it is I."
All except Peter were stricken dumb.
Peter said, "Lord, if it's You, bid me to come."
Jesus said, "Come," and Peter complied.
While walking toward Jesus, he became terrified.
Peter started to sink as he saw the waves soar;
All of his faith went right out the door.
Peter shouted with fear, "Lord, help me out!"
Jesus grabbed Peter asking, "Why did you doubt?
Peter, my friend, your faith is too small."
They got into the boat, and the Lord stopped the squall.

Repercussions from the Picnic

Jesus' miracle-picnic caused quite a human reaction,
And many sought Jesus as a free-food attraction.
Jesus said, "Through Moses, manna came from the ground,
But I am the Bread of Heaven come down.
From now on My flesh and blood are your food."
Then the crowd walked away in the grumbling mood.
Jesus asked His disciples, "Aren't you leaving too?"
Peter said, "Where would we go? Words of life come from You."

The Good Samaritan

A lawyer, a master of theology,
Asked, "How can I gain life eternally?"
Jesus replied, "What does the law tell?"
He said, "To love God and treat neighbors well."

"You're right," said Jesus, "You're right on track."
"But who is my neighbor?" the lawyer asked back.
The Lord's answer would be a surprise.
Jesus told him this story to open his eyes:
"A Jewish man was traveling one day
On the road from Jerusalem toward Jericho's way.
Then robbers came and stole all he had;
They beat the poor fellow and left him half-dead.
A rabbi and Levite both passed him by;
Then came a Samaritan, who let out a cry,
'O my poor fellow, what have they done?
And if I don't help, I'm the guilty one.'
He washed the man's wounds with oil and wine
And took him to an inn where he could recline.
He took care of the man, and on the next day,
He gave the innkeeper money to pay.
He said, 'I'll be back if that's not enough;
Please give him good care. These times are tough.'"
Jesus asked, "Who was the neighbor, which of the three?"
"The one who showed mercy." the man said thoughtfully.
Although Samaritans were despised by the Jew,
He showed mercy to one who could have been you.
Jesus summed up this story with only one aim,
"As you go forth, now do the same."

Parable of the Great Feast

A certain man prepared a meal so fine;
He invited his guests to come and to dine.
But they were so busy with pleasures and frets,
They told his servants to express their regrets.
One had a new field which he had to inspect;
One had a new wife whom he couldn't neglect.
Another had to check his new cattle.
The host thought these excuses sounded like prattle.
So he told the servants to go into the street
To invite the poor and all that they meet.

But the banquet hall still had more space;
Again the servants went out to fill up the place.
From the highways and byways the people poured in,
And then it was time for the feast to begin.
Jesus said it's important to consider the cost
Lest your place at the table forever be lost.

The Prodigal Son Parable

Christ taught of God's love through the prodigal son,
Who took his dad's money and left to have fun.
He spent it to party, and when the money was gone,
His friends disappeared and left him alone.
He ate with the pigs and started to cry,
"My own father's servants live better than I.
I am no longer worthy to be called his son;
Maybe he'll hire me if there's work to be done."
So he returned home where his father was waiting;
His father shouted with joy, "Let's start celebrating!"
He put a ring on his finger and a robe on his back;
"My son once was dead, and now he is back."

The elder son was fit-to-be-tied.
"That's just not fair," to the father he cried.
"What about me and all I have done?"
The father spoke kindly to his elder son,
"Son, you've been faithful in doing your chores;
All I possess has always been yours.
I beg you now to please come around,
For your bother was lost, and now he is found."

The Beggar and the Rich Man

There was a rich man who was splendidly dressed;
He lived sumptuously and had only the best.
A beggar, named Lazarus, lay by his doors
Begging for scraps while the dogs licked his sores.
One day both the beggar and rich man had died;

Lazarus' soul flew to Abraham's side.
The rich man's soul went to the place of hot fire.
He called out to Abraham, "Please grant my desire.
Just let Lazarus wet my parched lip
With a drop of water from his fingertip."
The answer he got was so hard to bear:
"You lived in comfort, but you didn't share.
Besides, the chasm is simply too great;
It is impossible to cross over the gate."
The rich man then begged, "Let Lazarus be sent
To warn my five brothers of this place of torment.
They'll surely believe one who returns from the tomb."
Abraham's answer showed it's not wise to presume:
"If they don't heed the prophets and all they have said,
They will not believe one who returns from the dead."

The Ten Bridesmaids Parable

Ten bridesmaids went for the bridegroom's returning;
All took their lamps with oil for burning.
Five wise bridesmaids were prepared for the wait
And took extra oil in case he arrived late.
But five foolish bridesmaids did not prepare
Then asked the others if they had oil to spare.
The wise bridesmaids said, "We can't give you more;
You must hurry and run to the store."
When they were gone, the groom came with a call;
The wise bridesmaids entered the big banquet hall.
When the foolish returned, they called at the gate,
But the door had been shut, and it was too late.
Jesus warned, "Being prepared is a lesson to learn,
For you will not know the hour I return."

The Woman at the Well

Jesus sat by Jacob's well and asked for some water.
The woman he asked was a Samaritan daughter.
She couldn't believe that a Jew would so sink

To talk to a Samaritan or ask for a drink.
"If you knew who I was, you'd ask Me for a drink."
The woman had no idea just what to think.
Jesus said, "I have water that will never fail."
"But sir," she replied, "You don't carry a pail,
But give me this water, so I'll never thirst."
Jesus said, "You must go call your husband first."
"I have no husband," the woman replied.
"That's true"; Jesus said, "you've already had five."
"I perceive you're a prophet, but we don't worship as you."
Jesus affirmed, "Salvation is of the Jew.
The time has come for a new worship to start;
True worship is spiritual and comes from the heart."
She said, "The Christ is coming to teach all things that be."
Jesus replied, "It is He that is speaking to thee."
The woman ran into town, to all people she knew,
"Come check out this man who knows all that I do."
Many Samaritans went to see if He could be the Lord.
And many believed because of His word.

The Parable of the Unforgiving Debtor

Jesus likened God's Kingdom to a certain king
Whose servant owed an amount most staggering--
Somewhere around ten million dollars or so;
That's what ten thousand talents were worth long ago.
So the king ordered that the servant's family be sold
And all his belongings be traded for gold.
The servant faced the king on his reckoning day
And begged for the king's patience until he could pay.
The king, moved with compassion as he heard his plea,
Forgave the whole debt and set the poor servant free.
After being relieved of a debt so immense,
He saw a co-worker who owed him one hundred pence.
One pence was the wage for one working day.
He grabbed the man's throat and demanded he pay:
"Pay me what you owe, and I want it now!"

The poor fellow answered, "I'll pay you; I vow."
But his co-worker's plea didn't change his decision,
And he had the poor fellow cast into prison.
The other servants were grieved and went straight to the king,
"The servant you pardoned has done a terrible thing."
When the king heard the story, he was appalled,
And the unrighteous servant was quickly recalled.
The king said, "I was happy to be generous with you,
But you've been too wicked to show kindness too.
The tormentors now will take you away,
And every penny you owe, you must repay."
"So likewise," said Jesus, "in torment you'll live
Until from your heart, you truly forgive."

The Pharisees

The Pharisees were the religious elite
Who thought they were better than the man on the street.
They knew the scriptures right from the beginning;
They loved their own goodness and avoided all sinning.
Don't you think the Pharisees would have been glad--
That Jesus was the best news they ever had?
Here was a man who fit to a tee
Every word which was spoken in prophecy.
Not for a minute! They had anger and fear.
Jesus tried hard to show them, but they wouldn't hear.

The Feast of the Booths

It was time to celebrate the Feast of the Booths
When Jesus went to the temple to reveal new truths.
Jesus' brothers scoffed because He went late:
"Why miss a chance to show off, Mr. Great?"
Jesus knew well that tension was brewing;
An untimely arrival could be His undoing.
The people were waiting with anticipation
When Jesus arrived for the big celebration.
Plans to arrest Him were bantered about;

Then on the last day Jesus stood up to shout:
"Come unto Me, for I have a supply
Of living water that shall never run dry.
Living water will flow from your belly within;
The time of the Spirit is about to begin."
The Pharisees ordered guards to arrest Jesus that day,
But after hearing Him speak, they wouldn't obey.
The Pharisees asked, "How could you be so deceived?"
Although the crowd was debating, many believed.

The Woman Caught in Adultery

The Pharisees were always trying to test Him,
Hoping He would mess up so they could arrest Him.
A woman caught in adultery was part of one plot
When the Pharisees tried to put Christ on the spot.
They caught the poor woman in the midst of the deed.
"The law says to stone her!" Jesus agreed.
Jesus said, "Who never has sinned may cast the first stone."
Soon, one by one, her accusers were gone.
Jesus cut through this matter, right to the core,
Then told the woman, "You are free; sin no more."

Jesus about Taxes

The Pharisees tried to trick Jesus again:
"Do you pay taxes? Do you bow down to men?"
Jesus picked up a coin so aptly designed,
Asking, "Whose image do you see enshrined?"
The crowd answered, "Caesar's!" without hesitation,
The emperor of the great Roman nation.
Jesus replied with an agreeable nod,
"Give to Caesar what's Caesar's; what is God's give to God."
Because of Jesus' clever retort,
The Pharisees found no offence to report.

The Sadducees' Question

The Sadducee Jews denounced resurrection,
So they asked Jesus this leading question:
"To Seven brothers a woman was married,
Each in his turn, as they died and were buried.
After she died, whose wife is she then?"
Jesus said, "Here it's different with women and men.
In heaven there is no need for marriage,
But don't be confused by this disparage.
It will happen just as God has said:
He will raise up the righteous after they're dead.
As God spoke to Moses through a burning bush,
When He gave Moses that life-changing push,
He described Himself and His identity
As being the God of the Ancient Three:
'I am the God of Abraham, Isaac and Jake.'
That proved to Moses He wasn't a fake.
He is God of the living, not of the dead,
Which means they're alive, just like God said."
"Well said, Teacher!" many expressed.
His answer put further questions to rest.

The Greatest Commandment

After Jesus brought the Sadducees to task,
A scholar had a fresh question to ask.
He was an expert, not very humble,
And was sure he could cause Jesus to stumble.
He asked, "What is the very greatest command?"
Jesus summed them all up so they could understand,
"Love the Lord God with all your heart, strength and mind.
In this are all of the commandments combined.
As you love yourself, you must love your neighbor;
It's kindness of heart, not works of duty and labor."

Jesus Confronts the Pharisees

Now Jesus asked them what seemed like a riddle,
Which put the Pharisees right in the middle:
"Who is the Christ; whose son is he?"
"He's David's son," they said confidently.
Jesus continued, since they were all in accord,
"But in the *Psalms* David calls Him his Lord.
If he calls Him Lord, how can the Christ be his son?"
The Pharisees were completely undone.

From that day on they had no more to say;
They would have to stop Jesus some other way.
Jesus is Truth, and Truth is not blind;
When Jesus saw evil, He spoke His mind.
Jesus saw the religious for what they were,
With their long-tasseled robes and hearts so impure:
"Woe to you Pharisees, you religious fakes,
You whitewashed tombs, you brood of snakes!
You claim to lead the people so well;
Instead you are leading them right into Hell.
At your hands all the prophets have died,
And you walk around full of self-righteous pride."

Nicodemus

Jesus' wise answers drove them further apart
Because He revealed their darkness of heart.
But there was one Pharisee, Nicodemus by name.
Hidden by night's darkness, to Jesus he came,
"You are from God we can all plainly see;
What is the answer to this mystery?"
Jesus answered his questions in the simplest way,
And these words are true to this very day:
"You must be born of the Spirit, born from above,
Starting brand new with God's Spirit of Love.
Just as the wind blows, filling up every space,
The Spirit goes to the heart that gives Him a place.

For God sent His Son, and if you believe,
Everlasting life you will surely receive."
Nicodemus wondered at Jesus' words clear and true,
And Jesus wondered at Nicodemus and how little he knew.

Jesus Heals and Reveals Blindness

There was a young man who was born without sight.
The disciples asked Jesus what caused his plight,
"Was it his or his folks' sin that made him blind?"
Jesus answered, "It was nothing of such a kind.
This is to show that I am the true light."
(This man was not the only one without sight.)
Then Jesus made a paste of spittle and clay,
Anointed his eyes, then said, "Wash it away."
The man came back from the pool, shouting with glee;
He was rejoicing, "I can see! I can see!"
The neighbors were baffled, and all they could say
Was, "Is this the same man who sat begging each day?"
So they asked the man, "How did this take place?
We want to know. Tell us now, face to face!"
"A man named Jesus made two small mud pies
With His spit and some clay and anointed my eyes."
They took the young man to the Pharisees' court
And showed them the man, and he gave his report.
"Whoever would heal on the Sabbath Day
Must be a great sinner," was all they could say.

The Pharisees asked the man's parents, "Is this your son?
Was he really born blind? How was this done?"
They said, "Yes, he's our son, and he was born blind.
Ask him what happened; he can speak his own mind."
His parents were afraid of being involved,
Lest their synagogue membership would be dissolved.
The Pharisees tried to make the young man confess
That Jesus was a sinner, even if God did bless.
The Pharisees told him to tell his story once more,

But he wouldn't do it since he'd told them before.
A heated discussion came quickly about.
The now-seeing man asked, "How can you doubt?
Only a man of God could give me new eyes;
Why don't you know this if you are so wise?"
"How dare you question our authority?
You're just a sinner," they said arrogantly.
The young man was cast out; the 'discussion' was done.
Jesus found him and asked, "Do you believe in God's Son?"
He said, "I want to believe. Lord, do You know who?"
"You have seen Him"; said Jesus, "He is speaking to you."
The man fell down to worship, saying, "Lord I believe!"
Jesus said, "I come as a light, so the blind can receive,
And those who think they can see might be made blind."
Some Pharisees heard this and were now in a bind.
"What about us?" Jesus answered their plea,
"You are in sin because you claim you can see."

Raising Lazarus

While Jesus was healing and raising the dead,
The religious elite were shaking their head.
"Who does He think He is, this carpenter's boy?
He breaks Jewish laws, we're up to His ploy.
He heals on the Sabbath, disregarding the day,
And eats with the sinners and leads people astray.
He pretends to be good, but He really is evil;
All of His powers plainly come from the devil."
Jesus' outrageous behavior stuck in their craw,
But the raising of Lazarus was the last straw.
God's Plan of redemption was to come to a head
When Jesus showed that He gives life to the dead.

Mary and Martha sent word that their brother was sick;
They needed Jesus and needed Him quick.
But Jesus delayed the trip for two days
And told His disciples this would end in great praise.

When He finally arrived, the two sisters cried,
"If you had been here, he would not have died."
For Lazarus, Jesus had tender devotion;
Then Jesus wept, overcome with emotion.
Jesus said, "Take Me to him," so they went to the cave.
He called, "Lazarus, come forth," and he walked out of his grave.
Then Jesus said to all those around,
"Unwrap his grave clothes so he won't be bound."
Jesus came to deliver from death and forgive:
"Believe in Me, though you die, yet shall you live."

People flocked to Jesus because of this miracle.
The religious elite were completely hysterical.
They now were serious about killing 'that man';
The time now had come to proceed with a plan.

The Final Week

For scripture to be fulfilled with perfect adherence,
It was time for Jesus to make his public appearance.
He set his face toward Jerusalem where it all must take place,
Where he would be praised and then die in disgrace.
Jesus told His disciples of what lay ahead,
But they did not comprehend one word that He said.
Now that He had revealed His kingdom of power,
He pressed on to Calvary, His final great hour.
His sinless, human blood was the only solution
That could wash away sin and give absolution.
If Satan had really known what He was about,
He would not have killed Jesus or made the mob shout.

Zacchaeus Climbs a Tree

As Jesus approached Jericho town,
News of His coming spread quickly around.
Zacchaeus was short and climbed up a tree;
He was excited, and he wanted to see.
When Jesus spotted Zacchaeus out on a limb,

He announced He would have supper with him.
The crowd's disapproval was very intense,
For he had made himself rich at the public's expense.
Zacchaeus immediately came down from the tree
And proclaimed to the crowd most joyfully,
"I'll give one half of my wealth to the poor,
And all I have cheated, I'll give back four times more."
Although Zacchaeus had been such a louse,
Jesus said, "Today salvation has come to his house;
The Son of Man came to save that which was lost."
Zacchaeus found the pearl that is well worth the cost.
Jesus left Jericho as He pressed toward His fate;
With the power of death, He had a pre-ordained date.

Jesus Heals Two Blind Men

A large crowd followed as Jesus set out.
Two blind men by the roadside started to shout,
"Lord, Son of David, have mercy on us."
The crowd was disturbed by such a big fuss.
They tried to hush them and make them behave,
But all the louder, they continued to rave.
Jesus stopped, "What are you asking of Me?"
They quickly replied, "Lord, we want to see."
Jesus touched their eyes, and their sight was restored.
The crowd joined them in praising the Lord.
Jesus continued His journey without much delay
To arrive in Jerusalem on the prophesied day.

Palm Sunday

Jesus sent His disciples to acquire a colt;
Then they covered the donkey's back with a coat.
As Jesus rode the colt through Jerusalem town,
People waved palms and gathered around.
They began to rejoice, praise God and to shout;
Had they been still, the stones would have cried out.
Later Jesus wept over this historical city,

His heart full of compassion and filled with great pity.
Jesus knew, one day, there would be great devastation
Because they missed the time of His visitation.

Cleansing the Temple

Then Jesus went to the temple and started to shout.
He raved as he cast the money changers all out:
"The temple was made to be God's house of prayer;
It's a den of thieves, and you don't even care."

Jesus Foretells the Future

Jesus and his disciples were at the temple site;
The poor widow had just given her famous last mite.
The disciples marveled at the massive stone wall.
Jesus announced, "Soon each stone will fall."
The disciples sought Jesus to ask privately,
"When will the end come; what will the signs be?"
Jesus explained to His small congregation
That these things will happen in the same generation:
"False prophets will come and cause great confusion.
It'll be a time of deception and great delusion.
The earth will see evil as never before,
With an increase of knowledge and rumors of war.
Kingdom against kingdom and nation against nation,
The world will suffer great tribulation.
Disease will run rampant, and famine will soar;
The seas will churn, and the waves will roar.
When you see earthquakes and signs in the sky,
It's time to look up, for your redemption draws nigh.
Iniquity will flourish, with men's actions depraved.
Only he who endures to the end shall be saved.
There'll be many offended, a sign of the time,
And speaking of Me shall be rendered a crime.
This age will not end till your assignment is done,
With God's Kingdom message preached to every last one.
False christs and prophets will arise everywhere;

You must know My word so you can beware.
Take heed, all those who like to party and drink,
Don't be caught unaware when the world starts to sink.
Watch, therefore, and stay always in prayer,
So you can escape and not get caught in the snare.
These warning signs must not be rejected;
My return will occur when it's least expected.
As in Noah's day, folks will not discern.
They'll be marrying and feasting when I return.
As you know by the fig tree when summer is near,
You can know the season when I'm soon to appear."
Jesus concluded with a clear metaphor,
"When these things happen, I am right at the door."

Anointed for Burial

Jesus and His disciples were invited for supper
At a home in Bethany of Simon the leper.
With no premonition or one word being said,
A woman came and poured oil on the Lord's head.
It was costly spikenard, fit for a master,
Stored in a jar made of white alabaster.
The disciples almost went into a rage:
"That woman just wasted almost a year's wage!
It could have been sold to help those in need."
Judas said that because of his greed.
Jesus explained, "I won't always be here.
I am being prepared for My death, which is near.
Her generous deed and the love that it shows
Shall follow the Gospel wherever it goes."

Judas, offended, slipped out the door
And went to the chief priests where he did implore:
"I know you want Jesus taken out of the way.
I'll lead you to Him. How much will you pay?"
"Thirty pieces of silver." Judas agreed,
Now to find the right time for his evil deed.

The Last Supper

The Passover feast was a yearly celebration
From the time of Moses when God delivered their nation.
Jesus had a special upper room set aside;
With His twelve disciples, it was time to confide.

Jesus Washes His Disciples' Feet

Jesus arranged the whole meal, and to make it complete,
He put on an apron to wash His men's feet.
Peter objected, "You cannot wash my feet now;
That is one thing I will never allow!"
Jesus said, "Peter, this is how it must be;
Unless I wash you, you can have no part with Me."
Such a horrible thought filled Peter with dread:
"Then Lord, wash my feet, my hands, and my head."
So Jesus washed their feet, every last one;
Then He explained what He had just done:
"As you see Me serve, you must serve all others.
You must do as I've showed you to all of your brothers."

Jesus Serves Communion

Each man took his place at the Passover Feast
To partake of the lamb and the bread without yeast.
Then breaking the bread, Jesus said, "Take this and eat;
This is My Body. Do this when you meet."
He took the wine, saying, "Drink, this is My blood;
To you this will always be spiritual food.
I will not drink of the fruit of the vine
Until we drink together when the Kingdom is Mine."

Judas' Betrayal

"It is My time, I must soon go away.
One of you now is going to betray."
All of the disciples started to cry,
"Oh My Lord, Is it I? Is it I?"

Judas asked that same question too,
And Jesus replied, "Yes, it is you."
As Jesus and His disciples continued their meal,
Judas left from their midst to get on with his deal.
He had to proceed in the darkness of night
When Christ's many followers were well out of sight.

Jesus' Farewell

Jesus said, "You must listen before I go away;
There is so much to tell you, so much to say.
I am in My Father, and you are in Me;
I go now to prepare many mansions for thee.
I have come not to judge, but to save the lost world;
This can only be done by receiving My Word.
I am the Way, the Truth and the Life.
(These words still cut the world like a knife.)
The world will hate you because of My name;
As they've treated Me, they'll treat you the same.
The Holy Spirit will come so you won't be alone;
You will find that you are no longer your own.
The Holy Spirit of Truth will be living inside
To be your teacher, comfort, and guide."

Jesus quoted from Zechariah a scripture that mattered,
"I will smite the shepherd, and the sheep will be scattered."
Peter assured Jesus, "For You I would die."
But Jesus warned Peter that three times he'd deny.

Gethsemane

The disciples had no idea of what Jesus was saying.
They adjourned to the garden for some serious praying.
Jesus beseeched them, "Help Me this watch to keep."
But His men became drowsy, and they all fell asleep.
Like sweat, drops of blood fell from His skin.
The work of redemption was now to begin.
As Jesus was suffering and in great agony,

He prayed, "If possible, let this cup pass from Me;
But, Father, I pray that Your will be done,"
For Christ was His perfect, obedient Son.
But Jesus was 'It'; there was no other plan,
No other option for the salvation of man.
Jesus knew the road before Him was tough
When He would face Evil and say, "That's enough!"
Judas entered the garden, giving Jesus a kiss,
With the Pharisees and scribes who were acting amiss.
With weapons the Roman soldiers gathered around.
When Jesus said, "I am He," they all fell to the ground.
Then Peter slashed off a servant's right ear.
Jesus placed it back on his head so he could hear.
Jesus told Peter, "Put your sword up,
For God has ordained that I drink from this cup."
Jesus spoke to the priests leading the mob:
"Why do you come with sword and with club?
Why now arrest Me in the darkness of night
When I'm at the temple everyday in plain sight?
But this is your moment, your time of gain,
When the power of darkness is permitted to reign."

Jesus' Trial

Like a sheep going to slaughter, Jesus followed 'The Way.'
His time had come, and He had to obey.
The Pharisees led Him to the Roman High Court;
No one could agree on the conviction report.
Jesus' disciples watched from afar,
Hoping no one would know who they are.
Jesus was never defensive; He simply stood mute.
The Roman Ruler, Pilate, who was very astute,
Said, "I wash my hands of this whole dirty deal."
Then to the mob he made an appeal:
"I find Him not guilty; set the poor fellow free."
The crowd accused Pilate of being Rome's enemy.
It happened so fast, this whole ugly scene;

Satan instigated the crowd to be ruthless and mean.
"Crucify Him! Crucify Him!" was their raging reply.
Jesus knew this was His Mission, and He had to die.

Judas' Demise

After Jesus' trial took its deadly course,
Judas Iscariot was filled with remorse.
He went to the temple, addressing the clan,
"I have betrayed an innocent man."
He threw the silver they paid him down on the floor;
The money he loved, he now did abhor.
"That's your problem," the priests and leaders replied.
Judas saw no way out but to commit suicide.

The Crucifixion

Jesus had been brutally whipped.
With a crown of thorns and flesh badly ripped,
Jesus carried the cross on Calvary's road.
An on-looker, named Simon, helped Him carry the load
To a place called Golgotha, the place of the skull.
Jesus was in this for the long haul.
The soldiers nailed his hands and feet to the cross;
The world was showing Him just who is boss.
His friends watched Him lifted with horror and dismay;
They never imagined things would happen this way.
On each side of Jesus two thieves were nailed.
By one of the thieves, He was quickly assailed,
"If you're the Messiah, then get us all off."
He mocked with the others and continued to scoff.
But the other thief gave out a cry:
"Jesus is innocent and He shouldn't die.
Remember me, Lord, as I'll soon close my eyes."
Jesus said, "Today you will be with Me in paradise."
While Jesus was suffering, the soldiers tossed dice
To bid for His robe that was seamless and nice.

Jesus cried, "Father, forgive them; they know not what they do."
(Like so many today, who don't yet have a clue.)
From noon till three, the day grew darker than night.
The mob and the soldiers were filled with great fright.
Jesus cried, "My God, My God, why have You forsaken?"
With the sins of the world, He had been overtaken.
Jesus, nearing the end, cried out, "I thirst."
They held a sponge to His mouth before His heart burst.
"It is finished!" Jesus triumphantly cried;
He gave up His ghost and then quickly died.
The Passover Lamb was now crucified.
Then a soldier pierced a spear into His side.

The veil in the temple split right in two;
The Old Covenant fulfilled, it was time for the New.
They took Jesus down, surprised He was dead.
The earth started to quake; they were all filled with dread.
Those who were watching all the things that were done,
Trembling said, "Truly this was God's Son."

Jesus could have called angels to set Him free;
He chose to lay down His life for you and for me.
Although Jesus had told them that this was The Plan,
His disciples got scared, and all of them ran.
After a mockery trial and no hesitation,
The Lamb of God bought our salvation.
For all of our sins, Jesus' blood was outpoured,
For He is our Creator, and He is our Lord.
"A tooth for a tooth, and an eye for an eye,"
His life for my life was why He chose to die.
Justice and mercy are father and mother,
And at the cross, the two kissed each other.
Our sin debt now paid by Jesus, God's Son;
The Promise fulfilled! The New had begun!

Jesus' Burial and Resurrection

A rich man named Joseph took Jesus away;
He wrapped Him in linen and put Him to lay.
He had hewn out a rock, which made Jesus' tomb,
And rolled a stone over to cover the room.
The leading priests heard that Jesus would rise
And sought to prevent such spreading of lies.
The Romans placed soldiers to guard the stone door
To prevent a deception and no rumors could soar.
Now as Jesus faced death, He took a great trip
Right into Hell, so He could break Satan's grip.
For three days Satan kept Jesus illegally,
But because He was sinless, Satan must set Him free.
Then power erupted as Jesus went back to the cave;
He took on a new body and came out of the grave.
Jesus now had the keys of death and of hell,
No longer just Lord, but now Savior as well.

Jesus Appears to His Disciples

When out of the grave, Jesus saw Mary Magdalene first.
When she realized it was Jesus, she wanted to burst.
She ran to the disciples, who were hiding in fear,
And told them that Jesus soon would appear.
While they were hiding away in a locked room,
Jesus walked through the wall and abolished the gloom.
Their reunion was filled with joy and delight;
Finally the apostles received understanding and sight.
Although Jesus had told them that these things must be,
Their eyes were opened, and at last they could see.
Jesus said, "It is I. See My hands and My feet;
Death is now conquered and the victory complete.
This is the time for great celebrations,
For the forgiveness of sins must be preached to all nations."

The Ascension

During a period of a full forty days
Jesus appeared to His disciples and taught of His ways.
"You must stay in the city and wait for the hour
When the Holy Spirit will come and fill you with power.
After that time, you will go forth
To lands east and west and to lands south and north.
I will be with you wherever you go;
You'll have My Spirit; that's how you'll know."
Jesus raised his arms to the Heaven so high;
His disciples watched as He rose up in the sky.
Then two angels in white, who made their hearts burn,
Said, "In the same way He left, He will return."

THE CHURCH AGE

The Holy Spirit Poured Out

One hundred twenty disciples assembled to wait,
Not knowing exactly the time or the date.
Ten days they waited, not counting the cost,
When the miracle happened called Pentecost.
For all of the disciples it was like a new birth
When God's Holy Spirit was released on this Earth.
He came as a wind and with fire and flame;
The followers of Jesus were never the same.
With power and love their souls fervently burned,
And they all spoke in languages they'd never learned.
They went out on the street to share the Good News,
For every man must have his own chance to choose.
Jerusalem was filled with people that day
From every nation and lands far away.
Some thought the disciples had too much to drink;
Peter rose up saying, "It's not what you think.
This is what Prophet Joel wrote about,
That God, one day, will pour His Spirit out."
Peter preached about Jesus and His crucifixion

And quoted from *Psalms* of the Lord's resurrection.
Hearing all this, the people were stung
As they miraculously heard, each in his own tongue.
Three thousand Believers were added that day;
The disciples of Jesus were well on their way.

The Acts of the Apostles

Peter Heals the Lame Man

Peter and John went to the temple to pray.
By the gate named Beautiful a lame beggar lay.
Peter spoke to the beggar and told him to look up;
He thought Peter had some coins for his cup.
Peter said, "Money is something that I have not,
But I can give something you haven't got."
He took the man's arm and then did proclaim,
"Arise and be healed in Jesus' name."
Instantly the lame man's feet were restored,
And he started leaping and praising the Lord.
As they entered the temple, everyone saw
That this was the lame man, and they were stricken with awe.
Peter said, "It's not through us this great thing was done,
But by the God of our fathers, through Jesus His Son.
The One you crucified, God raised from the dead;
Jesus fulfilled all that the prophets have said.
This is the One that Moses said would be sent,
But you can be forgiven if you repent."
When they heard these words, five thousand believed;
The priests of the temple were totally grieved.
They jailed Peter and John, just for the night;
In the morning they would decide what was right.

The rulers, elders and teachers all went
To sit in judgment of this strange event.
Peter told how Christ healed in a powerful speech.
Then the rulers told Peter he was forbidden to preach.
Peter answered, "That is completely absurd;

We speak only of things that we've seen and heard."
But there sat the healed man as pure evidence,
So the rulers and elders had no defense.
Finally Peter and John were sent on their way;
Then all Believers got together to pray:
"Lord, give us boldness, help us to proclaim;
May signs and wonders be done in Your name.
You've heard the threats the rulers are making."
After they prayed, the room started shaking.

Ananias and Sapphira

The Believers shared from the goods that they had;
Giving their money just made them glad.
There was a man, Barnabas, who sold all of his land,
Placing his money in the apostles' own hand.
They distributed the goods and passed them about,
And not one Believer was ever left out.
Ananias and Sapphira were husband and wife.
They made the biggest mistake of their life.
They sold their land and then made a bad call:
They kept some of the money but said they gave all.
Peter perceived this fateful deception,
This plot they devised from its inception.
Peter said, "Ananias, there was no need to pretend;
The money was yours to keep or to spend.
What you have done is greatly abhorred,
For you lied not to men but unto the Lord.
Whatever put such a thought in your head?"
At these words Ananias fell over dead.
Three hours later Sapphira came by,
And again Peter caught her in the same lie.
Peter said, "We just carried your husband outside."
Sapphira fell on the floor, and there quickly died.

The Apostles in Jail

The apostles drew crowds with their teaching and healing.
The jealous Sadducees were angry and reeling.

The Sadducees did not believe in a resurrection
And were not open to the slightest correction.
So they locked the apostles up in the jail
And set guards to watch so their plan would not fail.
That night an angel opened the prison door,
So the apostles could teach of resurrection once more.
The apostles hastened back to the temple court.
Then the Sadducees received the strangest report:
"The prison doors are still sealed and bound,
But not one apostle is there to be found."
They found the apostles out in plain sight
Teaching the Gospel with power and might.
They were taken to the high priest again.
Peter said, "We must obey God rather than men."
Gamaliel, who taught law and held great respect,
Spoke words of wisdom, strong and correct:
"If this movement originates merely from man,
With their leader dead, they will surely disband.
But if this movement is not of this sod,
You might find yourselves fighting with God."
The apostles were flogged and then were released;
As they suffered for God, their joy only increased.

The Stoning of Stephen

Terrible persecution came to Jerusalem City;
Stephen, a godly, young deacon, was stoned without pity.
He was preaching the Gospel and his face shone.
Before he died, he saw the Lord by His throne.
"Father, forgive them," he cried out loud.
A young Pharisee, named Saul, was part of the crowd.

Philip and the Ethiopian Eunuch

Christians fled from Jerusalem to a friendlier field,
Where they preached the Gospel, delivered and healed.
Philip preached in Samaria with power and might;
The miracles there brought much joy and delight.

Then an angel told him to go down Gaza Strip.
Philip saw a man in a chariot, making a trip.
He had been to Jerusalem to worship and pray
And was now headed back his homeward way.
He was an Ethiopian statesman, noble and proud;
From the book of Isaiah, he was reading out loud.
Philip ran over to ask him, "Do you understand?"
He answered, "How can I when I have no man
To explain the meaning of what has been said?"
Then Philip told about Jesus from the passage he read.
They came to some water and were really surprised;
"Look!" said the eunuch, "May I be baptized?"
So Philip baptized him that very day.
Then the Spirit of the Lord caught Philip away.
Philip found himself in Azotus, a city up north,
Where he preached the Gospel and then sallied forth.

Peter Heals and Raises the Dead

A short time of peace reduced the restraints,
So Peter traveled to Lydda to strengthen the saints.
A paralytic named Aeneas in Lydda did dwell.
Peter said, "Jesus heals you," and he was instantly well.
In Joppa a lady named Tabitha died.
Her lady friends grieved as they gathered and cried.
Tabitha was generous right to the core;
She sewed lovely clothing and gave to the poor.
Lydda and Joppa were close to each other,
So two men were sent to fetch Peter, their brother.
When Peter arrived he entered the room
And sent the mourners away, dispelling the gloom.
Peter immediately knelt down to pray
Then turned toward the bed where Tabitha lay.
Peter spoke to her saying, "Tabitha, arise."
The woman sat up and opened her eyes.
Peter presented the woman now fully alive.
Her friends rejoiced; the church continued to thrive.

Paul's Conversion

The growth of the Church was going so great
When the young Pharisee, Saul, stepped up to the plate.
He knew that this sect must be destroyed;
Every means that he could, he gladly employed.
He had the authority to put Christians in prison;
The high priest gave letters to support this decision.
Then to Damascus he journeyed one day
To capture the Christians who followed 'The Way.'
As he was proceeding on his 'high horse',
Something happened that changed his life's course.
Suddenly a light from Heaven shone all around;
The light was so bright, it threw Saul to the ground.
Then he heard a voice, though he could not see,
Saying, "Saul, why are you persecuting Me?"
"Who are you, Lord?" Saul asked on the road.
"I am Jesus, and you, Saul, are kicking the goad."
Then Saul cried out, "Lord, what would You have me do?"
From that moment on he was faithful and true.
Saul got up from the ground, but he'd lost his sight.
His men led him to town and found a place for the night.

Saul had a problem when he first believed;
The Christians suspected they were being deceived.
A Damascus disciple had a strange vision
In which God spoke and gave him a mission:
"Ananias, go to the house where Saul is staying;
Lay hands on him, for he has been praying.
When you do this, he'll get back his sight;
He'll preach to the weak and to people of might.
I've showed Saul in a vision what you're coming to do;
You'll find that Saul is waiting for you."
Ananias was nervous because of Saul's reputation,
But God put him at ease with this explanation.

It was as if scales fell from Saul's eyes.
Immediately he arose, and he was baptized.

Straightway he went to the town's Synagogue
And preached that Jesus is the true Son of God.
Many Jews wondered what got into Saul's head;
Some were so angry, they wanted him dead.
Barnabas told the apostles Saul's life-changing story;
The Church was relieved and gave God the glory.
(In the Mid-East he was called Saul,
But as a Roman, his name was Paul.
In Acts thirteen the name "Saul" is gone,
And he is called "Paul" from that point on.)

Moses and Paul; Grace and the Law

The Damascus Road was Paul's burning bush;
Like Moses, this gave his life a new push.
Paul once was caught up into the third heaven,
And here to him the full Gospel was given.
As on the mountain where God gave Moses the Law,
Paul was amazed at the things that he saw.
He learned the Gospel of Grace and received a great unction,
So he would know how the Church was to function.
The letters he wrote are the Church's foundation,
Like the Torah God gave to the Israel nation.
For the Law and Grace are two worlds apart:
Law deals with behavior; Grace deals with the heart.
The Law says we're guilty; Grace says we're forgiven,
But without the Law, Grace could not have been given.
Grace is the one thing no one can deserve;
Only by Grace are we made fit to serve.
By the Law all are lost, for it requires perfection;
Only the power of Grace brings true resurrection.
The Law was fulfilled the day Jesus died,
For the demands of the law were at last satisfied.
Adam's rebellion plunged the world into sin;
Through the kindness of Christ, we are made new again.
Moses wrote in the Old Testament; Paul wrote in the New,
For both the Law and God's Grace remain ever true.

Paul's Light Afflictions

Paul preached about Jesus with every breath;
Paul followed the Lord, many times facing death.
He planted churches like every apostle,
And he also encountered many a jostle.
He was whipped five times with thirty-nine lashes;
Once he was stoned, his body covered with gashes.
He suffered three shipwrecks and spent a night in the deep,
Often thirsty, hungry, and cold without sleep.
He simply called them his light affliction;
Spreading the Gospel was his only addiction.
His once-comfortable life, he said, was no loss;
It was gladly forgotten for the sake of the cross.
Those who carry God's Word often face persecution
And may suffer the ultimate, their own execution.
Paul knew that when these afflictions abated,
A glorious eternity for him awaited.

Paul at Philippi

While Paul was busy building God's Church,
The Lord never left faithful Paul in the lurch.
There was a girl who was demon possessed;
She heckled Paul daily until many were stressed.
With demonic power she had the gift to divine,
So for her owner she was a gold mine.
Paul finally spoke out, and the demon was nailed.
For this, Paul and friend Silas were beaten and jailed.
They were locked in a cell and chained to a rod.
Then what did they do? They sang praises to God!
All of a sudden there was a mighty earthquake,
Which made the prison doors open and shackles to break.
The jailer drew his sword to kill himself dead,
But Paul and Silas assured him no inmates had fled.
He was so grateful how the inmates behaved,
Trembling, he asked them, "How can I be saved?"
They replied, "Salvation is for your household and you;

Believe on the Lord Jesus; that's all you must do."
The jailer tended their wounds and took them home to be fed.
The whole family was baptized and then went to bed.
The next morning Paul and Silas were given release.
The jailer bade them farewell and said, "Go in peace."
"Wait a minute," said Paul to all those around,
"We're not about to slink out of town.
We were whipped and made a public disgrace
And demand an apology right to our face.
As citizens of Rome, you denied us fair trial."
When the officials heard this, they were not in denial.
They apologized quickly that they had done wrong
And begged Paul and Silas to quickly leave town.

Paul in Ephesus

As Paul cast out demons in Jesus' name,
The seven sons of Sceva tried doing the same.
They found a man who was demon possessed
And then proceeded with zeal and zest.
They took the man and started to shout,
"In the name of Paul's Jesus, demon, get out!"
But the demon was not about to comply,
And in protest he gave out a cry,
"I know Jesus and Paul, but who are you?"
Then he tore their clothes and beat them black and blue.
The news spread quickly about this event.
The Ephesians were stunned and were quick to repent.
The new believers saw their condition was dire
And burned their occult books in a public bonfire.
The large fortune of books which went up in flame
Displayed a deep reverence for the Lord's name.

More Drama in Ephesus

Paul taught, "Man made gods are not gods at all."
In Ephesus this teaching started a brawl.
A wealthy business man, named Demetrius,

Sold silver shrines of the goddess Artemis.
He called the craftsmen in his employ,
Saying, "Paul's teachings are sure to destroy
Our lucrative business of selling shrines.
We must stop Paul before business declines.
Artemis is worshiped through out our nation;
Paul's teachings will ruin her reputation."
The craftsmen could no longer stay quiet;
They were angry and ready to riot.
The believers forced Paul to hide out of sight;
He didn't like it but knew they were right.
The rioters attracted a sizable mob,
But the mayor of Ephesus was right on the job.
He settled the riot with this retort:
"If you have a grievance, you can take it to court.
Paul did nothing illegal, and as a consequence
We could break Roman law and have no defense."
The mayor's admonition settled the fray,
And the mob disbanded and went on their way.

Paul's Journeys

Paul traveled to Syria, Turkey, and Greece
And rejoiced as he saw God's kingdom increase.
He went to Jerusalem, obeying God in this mission,
Although he was warned he would end up in prison.
A mob tried to kill Paul, and he was arrested.
As a Roman citizen he loudly protested.
After two years of being detained,
The hostile environment only remained.
Paul knew he would not survive the ordeal,
So to Caesar in Rome he made an appeal.

Paul then had a dangerous journey to face
As he sailed to Rome to appeal his case.
He had given warning that the ship should not sail,
But the pleas that he made were to no avail.
After they left, a storm did arise;

For many days they saw no light from the skies.
Paul spoke up amidst all of the strife:
"The ship will be lost, but there'll be no loss of life."
Paul gave them instructions, although they seemed odd,
But by now they knew that Paul heard from God.
When the ship sank, they found their way to the shore;
They were all safe but chilled to the core.
They were graciously greeted by Malta barbarians,
Who built a big fire to warm the cold, weary ones.
Paul put sticks on the fire, and a snake bit his hand,
Which meant to the Maltans Paul was a bad man.
Paul shook off the snake, and should have been dead;
Now they thought he was deity instead.

The chief of the island gave them lodging to stay.
The chief's father was sick, so Paul went to pray.
With a miraculous healing, which was quickly revealed,
All who were sick went to Paul and were healed.
After three months it was time to depart;
The people gave them supplies so they had a good start.
Although Paul faced those many distresses,
He found that through trouble, God really blesses.
God's creative provisions kept Paul's spirit soaring.
(One thing we know, his life wasn't boring.)

Paul's Teachings

There are two sides to a coin, so we must learn
To know what is truth and how to discern.
Paul said God chooses the foolish and weak,
For God can supply all things to the meek.
Men are so quick to write their own rules;
In their own wisdom, they become fools.

The love of money is the deadliest weed
And the root of all evil, inspiring greed.
Money, itself, is a convenient material,
But it has implications that are totally spiritual.

Paul taught that we were in Christ when He died,
And our selfish nature must be crucified.
We were also in Christ when He was resurrected,
And by God's Holy Spirit, we are perfected.
Sin is no longer our burden and plight,
For we have passed from darkness to light.
In fact that's what baptism is all about;
The old man goes under, and a new man comes out.

We must set our affection on things above
And walk in forgiveness, power and love.
Love is the one power that never can fail;
Paul lived these truths whether free or in jail.
He taught that when the Holy Spirit comes to abide,
We'll have the fruit of the Spirit living inside.
The fruit, namely love, kindness and peace,
Joy and gentleness will grow and increase.
Of the gifts of the Spirit, we are to take heed;
These gifts will supply everything that we need.
We need words of wisdom and gifts to discern,
Gifts of healing and miracles, so much to learn.
The gift of prophecy we must not neglect;
We must give all of the spiritual gifts our respect.

There are many voices that try to deceive;
We must stay connected with those who believe.

Paul said, "Don't blame people when there is a problem
But powers of darkness which are able to prod them."
We are to bind evil spirits and cast them away,
To forgive the offender and constantly pray.
He taught we can put on the armor of God,
Clothed with God's light and with the gospel be shod.

God created "them" woman and man,
The very foundation of His family plan.

To prepare for a marriage that will endure,
A boy and a girl are to keep themselves pure.
A man is to be like Christ to his wife;
He must be willing to lay down his life.
The wife is to show her husband respect,
To treat him kindly and not to neglect.
On a path of wisdom, they're called to trod
And to train their children in the goodness of God.

Paul's Letters

The letters from Paul still serve the Church well,
Most which were written from a prison cell.
Today they exist in many translations:
To the *Philippians, Corinthians,* and the *Galatians.*
To the *Ephesians, Colossians, and to the Romans,*
The *Thessalonians, Titus, Timothy and Philemon.*
Paul was eventually was killed for his faith.
He had no fear, especially of death.
Paul wrote in *Philippians* before he was slain,
"To live is Christ; to die is gain."

James, Peter and John

To James, Peter and John we also are debtors;
They teach kingdom truths in their wonderful letters.
Peter's epistles tell of God's promises and power
And how to prepare for the great final hour.
John's first letter says love casts out fear,
And we must walk in the light with those who are near.
James says we must be quick to listen and slow to speak;
We must tend to the orphan and those who are weak.
He teaches that God's wisdom is peaceful and pure,
And when afflicted, with patience endure.
These letters cover so very much more,
And all give us marvelous truths to explore.

The Great Commission

The Church, the Believers, the Temple of God,
The Body of Christ now walk on this sod.
We are the salt and the light, His feet and hands.
We are commissioned to bring His Word to all lands.
Jesus Himself gave this awesome assignment,
Which we must heed to be in alignment.
We are to go forth in His name without fear
To show God is Love and that He is near.
Salvation's message we are called to proclaim
And to baptize those who trust in His name.
The power He's given is mighty indeed,
For we are also commissioned to meet every need:
To heal the sick, to raise up the dead,
To cast out the demons that fight in our head.
His blessings are to be passed to all generations
As the Word of God is preached to all nations.

The Believers' Tools

Our lives on this Earth are a battle and fight
Of good and evil and of darkness and light.
Jesus gave us His promise, His Word, and His power
So we could have victory in this very hour.
We need understanding and must not be blind,
For Satan is out to deceive all mankind.
We have weapons of warfare; the greatest is praise,
Which made walls tumble down in the ancient of days.
By speaking God's word, Satan must flee,
And through the blood of the Lamb, we have victory.
We must learn to trust God with every breath;
We must not love our lives, even to death.
All Believers who have made Jesus their choice
Have reason to praise, to sing, and rejoice.

THE END OF THE AGE

Although there is sorrow and struggle and death,
One day we all will draw our last breath.
Our choices determine the end of the story;
If we choose God, we have the promise of glory.

The Last Days

Paul wrote to Timothy that in the last days
Men will be selfish in all of their ways.
They will be scoffers, without natural affection,
No self-control and no sense of direction.
We read in chapter four of *First Thessalonians*
And in chapter fifteen of *First Corinthians*
That a great resurrection awaits all Believers,
And judgment and darkness await the deceivers.
This drama of life versus death one day will end;
Jesus the Lord will suddenly descend.
With a great shout, the trumpet shall blare;
We shall be caught up to meet the Lord in the air.
The dead in Christ shall be the first to arise;
Those still alive will meet Him in the skies
To be taken away to the mansions above,
A place of beauty, of light and of love.

Revelation

God showed John in a great revelation
Of future events and the great culmination.
Revelation is filled with much mystery,
With words spoken in symbols and allegory.
The Alpha and Omega appeared unto John,
The One Who was, is, and is yet to come.
His garment was girded with a gold sash;
His eyes burned with a fiery flash.
His voice was like waters crashing the shore,
And out of His mouth came a double-edged sword.

His hair was like snowy-white wool on His head,
And when He spoke, John fell down as dead.
He said, "Write the churches of the things that you see,
Of things that are now and things yet to be."
He told John in each letter just what to say;
These letters still guide us to this very day.

Letters to the Seven Churches

To The Church of Ephesus:
"You apply well your gifts to discern,
But you've lost your first love, a real concern.
The victorious ones will eat from My tree,
Securing their lives eternally."
To The Church in Smyrna:
"You are rich for you have stayed strong during strife.
You may face death, but you will never loose life.
Persecution will come; remain faithful and true,
And the crown of life will be waiting for you."
To The Church in Pergamos:
"You have stayed true when surrounded by sin,
But you've been lax about your members within.
The victorious ones will eat manna from Heaven,
And on a white stone their new names will be given."
To The Church in Thyatira:
"Your faith and charity are known well,
But there are some who heed Jezebel.
She has enticed them to be ruled by lust,
But I know your hearts, and My judgments are just.
Those who are strong and do not succumb
Will rule with Me in the world yet to come."
To The Church in Sardis:
"You think you're alive, but you are dead.
Truth hasn't mingled with your heart and your head.
It's time to wake up, casting off unbelief.
It will be too late when I come as a thief.
There are some who have kept their robes without stain,

So in the *Lamb's Book of Life* their names will remain."
<u>To The Church in Philadelphia:</u>
"I've put before you a wide, open door.
Your enemies will bow down on the floor.
Because you have not given in to denial,
I will keep you from the hour of trial.
Because you've held fast to the path that you trod,
You will be pillars in the temple of God."
<u>To the Church of Laodicea:</u>
"Be hot or cold, not a person of doubt,
But you are lukewarm, and I'll spit you out!
You think you are rich, but you're wretched and blind,
But you can still become as gold most refined.
Even now, I knock at the door of your heart;
If you ask me in, I will never depart.
My promises are for My people alone.
If you overcome, you will sit on My throne."

The Seven Seals

Then a door to Heaven opened so wide,
And John was invited to enter inside.
There sat God on a throne, encircled with light,
And twenty-four elders, wearing crowns, dressed in white.
There was a rainbow of emerald and magnificent color.
All bowed down in praise, giving God honor.
The time had now come to open the scroll,
But no one was worthy who could unroll.
John started to weep. Then the elders said,
"Here comes the Lamb that arose from the dead.
He's the Lion of Judah, heir of David the king."
When the Lamb took the scroll, they started to sing:
"Worthy is He whose blood paid the price,
Who for the people was the sacrifice."
Then every creature from Heaven to under the sea,
Ten thousands of thousands sang, "Glory to Thee."

There was noise like thunder when the Lamb broke the seal;
The future events He was about to reveal.
First, came a white horse to conquer the land;
The rider wore a gold crown with a bow in his hand.
The next seal brought a horse that was red;
The rider destroyed peace and brought war instead.
The third seal brought a horse that was black,
Whose rider brought famine, and all suffered lack.
The last horse was green; its rider was Death
With the power to kill one-forth of the earth.
With the fifth seal, John saw the saints that were killed;
They were told to wait till their numbers were filled.
The sixth seal brought a terrible earthquake;
Stars fell from the sky, causing mountains to break.
The Earth became still, as John describes,
Then four angels placed God's seal on Israel's tribes.
Seventh seal: Heaven was quiet for half an hour or so;
Then seven angels were each given trumpets to blow.
The prayers of the saints from God's altar arose,
Mixed with incense, filled up God's nose.
An angel cast down fire from the altar of God,
And thunder and lightening shook the earth's sod.

The Seven Trumpets

The angels were ready with their trumpets prepared,
And one by one each trumpet blared:
Trump One brought destruction to the grass and the trees.
Trump Two: A burning mountain fell into the seas;
One third of the sea life and ships were destroyed.
After this, Trump Three was employed.
A star named Wormwood fell from the sky,
And the water turned bitter, causing people to die.
Trump Four: The sun and moon lost one third of its light,
Affecting the day and also the night.
Trump Five: A fallen star unlocked the bottomless pit,
And scorpions and locusts arose out of it.

They stung those not wearing God's seal on their head.
Men didn't die but wished they were dead.
Trump Six released angels that made an army assemble,
Riding horse-like beasts that made men to tremble.
The army of men numbered two hundred million,
Dressed in armor of yellow, blue, and vermillion.
A third of all people were destroyed and smitten.
Then John heard seven thunders which were not to be written.
John was given a book, which he was told to devour,
And just like Daniel, his stomach turned sour.

The Two Witnesses

God will send two witnesses in Earth's final hour;
Like Elijah and Moses, they'll display awesome power.
For the first three and a half years of the great tribulation,
These prophets will speak God's word to each nation.
The words from their mouths will be fire-filled;
Those who would hurt them will by that fire be killed.
After they say all that needs to be said,
A beast ascends from the pit, striking them dead.
For three-and-a-half days the world will rejoice
Because the beast had the power to silence their voice.
Then on the third day, from death they'll arise;
As their enemies watch, they'll ascend to the skies.
An earthquake ensues; seven thousand are slain;
Then the Last Trumpet sounds, announcing Christ's reign.

The Woman in Heaven

John saw a woman in heaven with twelve stars in her crown
And a red dragon whose tail dragged down
One third of the stars which he threw to the earth.
This woman I saw was about to give birth.
The woman delivered a sound baby boy,
And the dragon was there to devour and destroy.
But the boy child was snatched up to God;
One day He will rule with his iron rod.

When the dragon found himself cast to the earth,
He persecuted the woman, the one who gave birth.
The earth protected the woman the dragon abhorred,
So he made war with her offspring, those who follow the Lord.

Two Beasts and the Dragon

Then John saw a beast arise out of the sea;
The dragon gave him his power and authority.
He had ten horns, just as Daniel had said,
But here he also has seven heads.
The beast received a wound to one head.
He miraculously appeared to rise from the dead.
For forty two months he blasphemed all things of God
And had power to rule all who lived on this sod.
The world was taken in by this master deceiver,
Requiring patience and faith for every Believer.
Another beast came out of the land
With a voice of a dragon and powers so grand.
He had powers to do miracles of evil,
Powers which come from the dragon, the devil.
He is called the False Prophet, and in unity
With the dragon and beast, made a new trinity.
He had a statue made of the beast from the sea
And gave it power to talk, miraculously.
The statue demanded to have total lordship,
And all peoples and tribes were commanded to worship.
Those not in the *Book of Life* did comply;
Those refusing to worship were sentenced to die.
People were not allowed to buy bread
Without the beast's mark on their hand or their head.
Then God sent three angels to give one final warning
And to speak to the saints of their future adorning.

John saw Israel's tribes who were marked with God's seal,
One hundred forty-four thousand, as the scriptures reveal.
They stood on mount Zion before the throne of the King

And sang a new song which they only could sing.
They were the firstfruits, redeemed from all man,
To be a pure offering to God and the Lamb.

The Seven Bowls (or Vials) of Wrath

John heard a great voice in heaven arise:
"It's time to pour God's wrath from the skies."
The angels took the bowls, seven being the sum;
For the wicked on earth, judgment finally had come.
Those who did not seek the forgiveness of sin
Received painful sores all over their skin.
The seas turned to blood, causing all fish to die;
The sun got too hot, and darkness filled up the sky.
The Euphrates River dried up, preparing the way
For the kings to assemble for that fateful day.
Three demons went forth from the dark trinity
To gather kings from each nation in unity.
Armageddon is named as their gathering place
Where the kings and their armies meet God face to face.

Christ Comes as a Thief

"Behold:" Christ said, "I come as a thief!"
Those who are ready are removed from the grief.

The Fall of Babylon and the Harlot

An angel poured out his bowl, the very last one.
A voice spoke from heaven and said, "It is done."
There was an earthquake like never before,
With lightening and thunders that let out a roar.
Huge hail stones fell from the skies,
Each about sixty-five pounds in size.

I saw a woman in scarlet sitting on the red beast.
From the blood of the martyrs she enjoyed her feast.
She is the Mother of Harlots and Abominations.

She seduced the kings and people of nations.
The harlot is the Bride's counterfeit,
All false religions that come from the pit.
The seven heads of the beast were her mountains of power.
The ten horns on the beast were the kings of that hour.
These kings surrendered, bowing their knee,
And gave to the beast their authority.
The kings destroyed the harlot and burned her with fire.
God allowed all evil to fulfill its desire.
A mighty angel announced from the skies,
"It's time for Babylon's fateful demise.
She lived in pride and gave herself glory.
In sorrow and torment she shall finish her story."
Babylon collapsed and turned into rubble.
The world experienced unbelievable trouble:
No more silver, gold or linen so fine,
No more vessels of ivory, oils or wine.
Alas, that great city where goods could be bought,
In one hour of time, has all come to naught.
No more music, laughter, and echoes of mirth,
For the blood of God's servants was found in the earth.

The Lamb's Wedding Feast

The rejoicing in Heaven burst forth like a roar,
"Hallelujah and praise to the One we adore!"
The bride, dressed in white from the greatest to least,
Has made herself ready for the Lamb's wedding feast.
The wonders of Heaven no man can describe.
There'll be people in Heaven from every nation and tribe.
There'll be families and loved ones, sisters and brothers,
Grandmas and grandpas, fathers and mothers.
There'll be a wedding feast at the great banquet hall,
And Jesus, the Bridegroom, will serve one and all.

Armageddon

One named Faithful and True came on His white steed,
And He went forth into battle, taking the lead
With all of His saints, each on a white horse,
To stop the beast and his prophet from their evil course.
He wore many crowns and a robe dipped in blood;
In Heaven He's known as "The Word of God."
On His vesture were written these words:
KING OF KINGS AND LORD OF LORDS.
The world's kings and their armies were gathered *en force*
To make war against Him who sat on the horse.
Out of His mouth came a sharp sword,
And He struck down the nations by His Holy Word.
All of humanity who took the mark of the beast
Were eaten by vultures, a horrendous feast.
The beast and his prophet were cast into the fire,
Whose flames will never grow weary or tire.

The Millennium

There will be the Millennium, one thousand years long,
When Satan is bound so he can do no wrong.
Into a bottomless pit, he will be cast;
For one thousand years his confinement will last.
The godly who suffered in the great tribulation
Will rule with Christ over every nation.
Then Satan will be loosed, again free to deceive;
People can choose to rebel or believe.
After Satan is freed, there will be one final clash;
And then all rebels will die by a lightening flash.

The Great White Throne Judgment

When this time is over, judgment begins,
A time when the world faces her many sins.
As Jesus warned, there is nothing concealed;
All things done in darkness will be revealed.

The fearful, immoral, those who practice a lie,
The sorcerers, and idolaters will all have to die.
For the haters of God, the future is dire;
They'll follow Satan, their leader, into the great Lake of Fire.
Those who allowed Christ's blood to atone
Will never appear before God's judgment throne.
Instead they receive their eternal reward
For accepting salvation and loving the Lord.
However Believers who wasted their day
Will see their deeds burned as stubble and hay.

The New Jerusalem

The old Heaven and Earth will all pass away;
A new Heaven and Earth will then come to stay.
The New Jerusalem will come down from above,
Christ's Holy City filled with joy and love.
Christ Himself will then take David's throne,
And He'll be surrounded by all of His own.
There'll be no more night because Jesus the Son
Is the Light which will embrace everyone.
There'll be no more death, sorrow or sighs;
Jesus Himself will wipe all tears from our eyes.
All stages of history will be complete,
And all of God's children will sit at His feet.
The Earth will be pure, just as it started
With millions of people, all the pure-hearted.
With redemption complete, the redeemed will now sing,
"Life is victorious, and death's lost its sting."

The angel told John, "Write these words for that day.
Blessed are they who believe and obey.
Let man continue to do his own will.
Let the evil become more evil still.
Let the righteous stay holy and pure
And walk in holiness as they endure"

Jesus spoke, "I am the beginning and end.
I will accomplish all I intend.
Blessed are those with robes washed from stain,
But outside the gate will the wicked remain.
I come with reward; you reap what you sow.
I've sent my angel so you would know.
Surely I come; it will not be long."
He will come for His bride who is vibrant and strong.
The bride now awaits, not knowing when,
Saying, "Even so, come, Lord Jesus. Amen."

The Finale---The Beginning!

Before the world was created, the Word was with God.
The Word became flesh and traveled this sod.
This Word, who is Jesus, dwelt among men,
So we could be His and be whole once again.
Through the living Word, Jesus, all things were made.
And by His shed blood, our transgressions were paid.
He is our Life, our Light and our Love.
We know that God loves us for He came from above
To teach us and tell of all He has planned,
For our lives are eternal and our future is grand.

The grace of the Lord Jesus Christ be with you all. Rev. 22:21